Roads Full of Idiots

Roads Full of Idiots

Asha

Published by Asha, 2024.

ROADS FULL OF IDIOTS

First edition. November 22, 2024.

ISBN: 979-8230265566

Written by Asha.

'On Kenyan roads, it's not just about getting from point A to B, it's about surviving the journey with a sense of humor, a strong suspension, and a whole lot of patience.'

— Asha, *Roads Full of Idiots*

Introduction

Kenya's road network is a masterpiece of organized disorganization, a patchwork quilt of highways, single lanes, bypasses, dual carriageways, and what can loosely be called pedestrian lanes. On paper, it's an intricate system designed to get people and goods from point A to B efficiently. In practice, it's a chaotic symphony of honks, potholes, and improvisation.

Yes, we drive on the left, well, theoretically. While the law books insist on it, the reality is far more flexible. The side of the road you drive on depends on three things: urgency, creativity, and how much you trust your vehicle's suspension. Pedestrian lanes exist, but they're often colonized by hawkers, wandering goats, cows, and more often than not bodaboda and Matatu using them as overtaking lanes.

Driving schools and licenses are supposed to be the golden ticket to mastering the roads, right? There's a system, exams, certifications, and of course, a shiny license card to prove you've earned your stripes. But let's be real here: the theory test barely scratches the surface of what happens when the rubber hits the road in Kenya. It's a bit like showing up to a cooking class and being asked to roast a chicken, but the only skill you've got is knowing how to microwave leftovers. The reality? The real driving lessons happen on the streets. Enter the seasoned Matatu driver who's been around long enough to know how to handle anything from a traffic jam to a herd of goats blocking the road. The most valuable driving school in Kenya isn't a licensed institution but a high-speed apprenticeship in a Matatu, where you don't just learn to drive, you learn to survive.

Take, for example, the Tout, to, Driver Program. This isn't your traditional 'learner driver' experience. Oh no. Here, the Tout, the same person who's been yelling at pedestrians to get into the Matatu becomes the driver for the hour, learning the ropes in the most unconventional of ways. Imagine this: the driver pulls over for tea or lunch (because, naturally, it's a five, minute affair). But instead of parking and relaxing, they throw the keys at the nearest Tout, who has just enough driving knowledge to get the Matatu around the block.

This is the moment when the Tout becomes the driver. They've spent hours watching the seasoned pro behind the wheel, memorizing the moves and tactics, knowing exactly when to swerve, brake, or honk like a maniac. Now, it's their time to shine. They start the engine, grip the wheel with the intensity of someone fighting for their seat in the Matatu, and begin what will surely be the most unpredictable 'driver training' session in history.

Of course, they've only been shown the basics. There's no formal curriculum here. It's all about the 'being given a squad' the unspoken code passed down from driver to Tout, with one main lesson: survival of the fittest. If the Tout can get the Matatu back to the terminal without too much drama and with passengers still alive, then they've earned their seat behind the wheel for the next day round.

And this training is surprisingly effective. After a few bumpy rides around the block, the Tout starts feeling the rush, knowing how to manage the accelerator with the delicate touch of a traffic cop at a very festive family reunion. They have a knack for dodging potholes, slaloming through pedestrians, and stopping just close enough to the curb to avoid a scolding (but not quite close enough to make it a full stop).

But this informal system comes with its own set of hilarious realities. When the driver returns from his tea break, he might find his 'student' confidently navigating the congested streets with newfound bravado. The passengers, meanwhile, have no choice in the matter, they're stuck in the Matatu, and their only goal is to reach their destination, no matter who's behind the wheel. Most are either ignorant of the exchange or simply too focused on getting where they're going to care about the driver's credentials. And even if they did notice, who are they going to complain to? The Tout? The driver? They could try, but the response would be simple: 'If you don't like it, get out. Just make sure you pay your fare before you go.' Whether they get to their destination in one piece or are stranded somewhere along the way doesn't really matter, it's all about paying your fare and hoping for the best.

The beauty of it all? Most of the Matatu drivers and Touts, turned, drivers will come out of this process unscathed, having learned to survive Nairobi traffic with an unsettling confidence, if not an actual understanding of road signs or traffic laws. What's the most important thing they've learned? How to bribe the traffic cops to keep the show on the road?

So, when you see a Matatu driving at the speed of a wildly successful escape artist, remember, it wasn't learned in a classroom. It was learned through 'Squad' training, with a whole lot of street, smart innovation. And no, the license you're holding doesn't really matter in this world; the real qualification is the ability to dodge a pothole, avoid a goat, and maybe take a few shortcuts along the way.

And then there are the roads themselves. Highways promise swift travel, but only if you manage to avoid the tractor in the fast lane and the cow casually grazing on the median. Single, lane roads are intimate affairs where overtaking becomes an act of bravery and prayer. Dual carriageways are a step up, but even they aren't immune to random jaywalkers who treat speeding cars as if they're moving in slow motion. Recently there are bypasses, the supposed relief valves for urban congestion, often transform into racetracks or experimental parking lots during peak hours. And as for the potholes? They're the real traffic managers, more like cratered monuments to our resilience, ensuring no one gets anywhere too quickly.

And then there's the holy trinity of chaos: Matatus, Bodabodas, and pedestrians. Matatus are rolling discos, Bodabodas are fearless stunt bikes, and pedestrians are masters of dodging vehicles like it's an Olympic sport. Go to the coast, enter the TukTuk, a three, wheeled, covered marvel that defies all expectations. They zip through traffic like bees, buzzing on narrow streets and squeezing into gaps no sane driver would consider.

Now sprinkle rain into this concoction, and chaos takes on a whole new meaning. Traffic halts, fares triple, and TukTuks, Matatus, and Bodabodas compete in a wet, muddy circus of survival. Kenyan roads aren't just a transport system, they're a vibrant, unpredictable ecosystem where humor, resilience, and sheer ingenuity keep the wheels turning.

Prologue

In Kenya, driving is an art form of chaos, a daily test of endurance, creativity, and a dash of good fortune. From the bustling streets of Nairobi to the winding roads of the countryside, navigating the traffic here is an adventure like no other. The road network, a mix of highways, single lanes, and bypasses, is a masterpiece of organized disorganization. It promises a smooth ride but often delivers a symphony of honking, potholes, and the occasional surprise a goat in the middle of the road, a Matatu driving the wrong way, or a motorbike squeezing through spaces you didn't think were possible.

You see, in Kenya, the rules of the road are more like suggestions, rules that are often bent or ignored entirely. While the law says we drive on the left, that left is really just the side of the road where you happen to find the least amount of traffic. If the right side looks clearer, well, why not use it? After all, who's going to stop you? Not the Matatu driver who's clearly in a rush to deliver his passengers and the loud music blaring from his stereo, nor the touts who've learned that survival on these streets requires more than just a license, it requires street smarts.

And then there are the streets themselves. From highways that somehow become parking lots, to bypasses that turn into racetracks at rush hour, you never quite know what you're going to get. Throw in some rain, and what was a road now becomes a survival challenge. The potholes are the true masters here, craters that define the path forward. They manage traffic better than any road sign could forcing everyone to slow down and navigate with care. But even then, the dodging doesn't stop: there are pedestrians darting across the road, Bodabodas weaving in and out of lanes like acrobats, and Matatus playing their own game of chicken, always a little too close for comfort.

This is Kenya's traffic world, a world where you learn to survive through trial, error, and a whole lot of honking. It's a place where driving schools might teach you the basics, but the real lessons come from getting on the road and figuring it out as you go. And, if you're lucky enough, maybe you'll even get a taste of what it means to be a Matatu driver or a tout. You'll learn quickly that there's no such thing as a perfect road. There's only the road ahead and the wild ride it promises.

ROADS FULL OF IDIOTS

Chapter 1: Matatu Madness

If you've never ridden in a Matatu, you haven't truly experienced Kenyan roads. These glorified minibuses are more than just a mode of transport; they're a cultural phenomenon. Each Matatu is a kaleidoscope of blaring music, flashy graffiti, and an atmosphere where rules are mere suggestions and speed limits are vague memories.

The first thing you notice about a Matatu is the exterior. No two Matatus are alike. Some are decked out in neon lights that could rival a Las Vegas casino, while others boast massive portraits of hip-hop legends, complete with inspirational quotes like, 'No Stress, Just Vibes.' It's as if the more outrageous the design, the faster the Matatu believes it can go.

Inside, it's an entirely different story. You're greeted by music at a decibel level that could wake the dead. One moment, you're being serenaded by Bob Marley; the next, you're in a rave with EDM beats that make your heart race faster than the speeding Matatu. The tout (or conductor), often a young man with the swagger of a rapper, shouts out destinations in rapid-fire Swahili, promising you'll get there 'faster than the wind.' He neglects to mention you might lose a few years of your life in the process.

Getting into a Matatu is an art form. Forget about orderly queues. It's a survival of the fittest scenario where sharp elbows and quicker reflexes determine who gets a seat. Once inside, the conductor starts his circus act, squeezing five people into a row meant for three. 'Shukisha hapo mbele!' someone shouts when their stop approaches, and the entire Matatu groans as everyone has to shuffle to let them out.

Then there's the driving. A Matatu driver isn't just a driver; he's a stuntman, a racer, and an illusionist all rolled into one. He'll overtake on blind corners, swerve around potholes with the precision of a

Formula 1 driver, and squeeze through gaps that defy the laws of physics. Traffic lights? Optional. Speed bumps? A mild suggestion.

But perhaps the most thrilling part is when a traffic police officer flags the Matatu down. The driver slows just enough to give the officer a hopeful look, and if they're in luck, they get waved through. If not, the whole vehicle collectively sighs as the driver and tout perform the 'fine negotiation dance,' a ritual involving wads of cash and handshakes.

If a Matatu has an accident with another car, regardless of whether it's a fender bender or a full-on collision, it's always your fault. If they hit them from behind, they'll tell you, 'You braked too hard, you're too slow.' You'll be asked to pay for the damages, and if you even think about getting the police involved, think again. There's no number to call, no one to turn to for help. It's pure luck if a cop shows up before the situation escalates. By the time that happens, the Matatu driver, the Tout, and a handful of random bystanders who suddenly appear will have surrounded your car. Their only goal is to harass you into paying up, as if you're the one who needs to be taught a lesson. And don't even try asking for time or space they're in a rush. They don't have time for accidents, just the next passenger and the next fare. You're stuck, and it's either hand over the cash or pray for a miracle, a cop who's actually around and willing to help.

As I sat squished between a student clutching a massive backpack and a grandmother balancing a live chicken on her lap, I realized something: in a Matatu, you don't just travel, you experience life in fast-forward. And if you're lucky enough to survive, you'll have a story worth telling.

And yet, for all the chaos, there's something endearing about Matatus. They're the lifeblood of Kenya's roads, a place where strangers laugh together over shared frustrations and where, despite the madness, everyone somehow gets to their destination.

ROADS FULL OF IDIOTS

Welcome to Matatu Madness. Buckle up or don't as seat belt isn't there. It's going to be a wild ride.

Chapter 2: Bodaboda Ballet

If you've ever set foot in Kenya, you've likely encountered the Bodaboda, the country's infamous motorcycle taxis. These two, wheeled warriors zip through traffic like stunt doubles in a never-ending action movie. They defy logic, physics, and occasionally gravity itself, all while ferrying anything from anxious office workers to a goat casually chewing cud on the backseat.

To call Bodaboda riders fearless is an understatement. These riders move with a reckless grace that teeters somewhere between genius and madness. Picture this: a rider balancing a full sack of potatoes on one side, a mattress on the other, and a passenger sandwiched in between. It's not transport, it's performance art.

But let's not kid ourselves: Bodaboda riders are a mixed bag. For every rider who glides through traffic with the precision of a surgeon, there's another who seems to believe red lights are optional suggestions and roundabouts are racetracks. Their uncanny ability to materialize out of nowhere, honking like they own the road, is both impressive and mildly terrifying.

Bodabodas are the ultimate multitaskers. They'll deliver packages, pick up your forgotten groceries, and, in emergencies, even serve as ambulances. They're a lifeline for many Kenyans, especially in rural areas where other transport options are scarce. Need to get to the next town in record time? A Bodaboda will get you there faster than you can say 'hold on tight' and you better hold on tight. Because if you don't, you might end up in the same pile-up that happens when drivers and pedestrians alike are left playing a game of survival in the middle of an open road.

In neighborhoods like Kawangware, where many residents earn less than five dollars a day, Matatus are the primary mode of transport.

Walking is often the other option, but for those fortunate enough to afford it, a Bodaboda is the next best thing. However, using a Bodaboda can feel like a luxury unless you're willing to share the ride with four other people because the more, the cheaper, right? Morning and evening rush hours are the worst times for Bodabodas, as the streets become clogged with riders, zipping in and out of traffic like a swarm of bees. Counting them is pointless; there's simply too many, and they don't seem to stop for anyone especially not for traffic police.

Even when the police are on duty, trying to control the madness at busy junctions, Bodaboda riders ignore the law with reckless abandon. When the officer signals 'go,' it's like a green light for Bodabodas to keep weaving through cars, as if the road is their own private racetrack. It's complete chaos, a dance of bikes and cars all moving at once with no regard for order.

In the coastal towns, where the sandy streets and salty air add a touch of drama, the Bodaboda culture takes on an even wilder edge. Riders dart between sluggish TukTuks and tourists armed with selfie sticks, leaving a cloud of dust and bemusement in their wake. It's a chaotic dance of survival where everyone seems to know their part except the tourists, of course.

And when it rains? Forget about it. The Bodaboda ballet turns into an extreme sport. Roads morph into mudslides, and the riders ever resourceful become human amphibians, splashing through puddles like they've been training for the Olympics. The irony? Fares double because, as they'll explain with a straight face, 'Rain is dangerous.' Dangerous for you, maybe not for them.

The reality of the Bodaboda industry is much darker. Many riders work long hours for meager pay, navigating treacherous roads and an almost complete disregard for safety. Helmets, if present, are often decorative, and passengers are left to place their faith in nothing but the rider's experience and the motorcycle's battered brakes.

Bodabodas, while indispensable to many, are also a ticking time bomb on Kenya's roads. Their reputation for reckless driving has made them infamous, and the consequences are often devastating. At Kenyatta National Hospital, there's even a reserved ward for Bodaboda riders injured on the roads, many of them lying in pain with fractures or amputations. These wards are a grim testament to the dangers of their trade. Riders' ignorance or outright disregard for helmets and other safety gear has caused countless young lives to be lost prematurely. It's a tragedy that extends beyond riders; passengers, too, often find themselves injured and left destitute after accidents, as most Bodaboda riders lack proper insurance coverage. And if the rider is lucky enough to escape injury? They'll disappear from the scene, leaving their victims to deal with the fallout.

The situation is even worse if you're driving a car and happen to get involved in an accident with a Bodaboda. Regardless of the circumstances, you'll almost always be at fault at least in their eyes. Within moments, riders from nowhere will swarm your car, hurling accusations, threatening to beat you, burn your vehicle, or worse. It's mob justice at its ugliest, and reasoning is rarely an option. The presence of the police, which should ideally bring order, often makes things worse. Many officers, in a bid to resolve the matter quickly, will side with the riders, reasoning that the car owner can afford to pay, even if they're not at fault. This skewed perception leaves drivers feeling helpless, caught in a system where survival sometimes depends on how fast you can pay or pray.

Bodabodas may be a lifeline for many Kenyans, but they are also a dangerous force on the roads. Their role as a vital means of transport is undeniable, yet the risks they pose to themselves, their passengers, and other road users are just as significant. It's a delicate balance of necessity and peril, one that continues to play out on Kenya's roads every single day.

Yet, for all their flaws, Bodabodas are a vital cog in Kenya's transport machine. They're flawed, fearless, and occasionally infuriating, but they're also indispensable. Behind the jokes and ironic observations lies a deep truth: The Bodaboda is not just a motorcycle; it's a symbol of Kenya's unrelenting drive to keep moving, no matter the odds.

Love them or loathe them, Bodaboda riders are here to stay, dancing through traffic, dodging potholes, and keeping Kenya's roads as lively, unpredictable, and resilient as the people who travel them.

Chapter 3: The Traffic Jam Chronicles

In Kenya, traffic jams or jams as we call them aren't just an inconvenience. They're a lifestyle. A rite of passage. A shared national experience that unites us in frustration and bemusement. To live in Kenya is to know that the phrase 'I'm stuck in traffic' is not just an excuse but a valid explanation for being hours late.

Traffic here is more than cars standing still. It's a vibrant, chaotic ecosystem, teeming with characters, commerce, and drama. Picture this: you're stuck on a stretch of road that hasn't moved in 30 minutes. A Matatu, with its blaring music and graffiti screaming 'Nairobi Hustler,' inches forward like a defiant turtle. Bodabodas weave through the stationary vehicles, honking at everyone and no one. Somewhere, a driver furiously revs their engine, as if sheer willpower will part the sea of cars.

And then there are the hawkers. Oh, the hawkers! These entrepreneurs see opportunity where others see gridlock. In a Kenyan traffic jam, you can buy anything and everything. Boiled eggs with Kachumbari (tomatoes, onions and coriander) and some sort of sausage? Absolutely. Fresh fruit, candy, or bottled water? No problem. Socks, steering wheel covers, phone chargers, wipers? You got it. Need a copy of last month's bestseller or a random self-help book with a title like How to Become a Millionaire in Three Days? They've got you covered.

It's not just goods; it's entertainment, too. While you wait for the cars to inch forward, you'll witness full-blown soap operas unfolding around you. Hawkers haggling with buyers over a 10, shilling discount. A couple arguing in the car next to you, windows down, audience engaged. A street preacher with a megaphone warning every one of the impending apocalypse, conveniently ignoring the fact that the jam itself feels like the end of days.

In these moments of forced immobility, Kenyans reveal their resourcefulness. Matatu passengers strike up conversations with strangers, debating politics or soccer like old friends. Drivers lean on their car doors, catching up on neighborhood gossip or lamenting the state of the roads. Some just sit silently, scrolling through their phones, while others blare music loud enough to turn the jam into an impromptu street party.

But the real most valuable players of the Kenyan traffic jam are the Jua kali mechanics who magically appear when a car inevitably breaks down. With tools that look like they've seen better days, they work their magic on the spot, often fixing things faster than you'd think possible. Payment is immediate, cash or mobile money called Mpesa, because in Kenya, the hustle never waits.

And let's not forget the police officers tasked with 'managing' the traffic. Armed with whistles and batons, they valiantly attempt to impose order on the chaos, though their efforts often result in more confusion. Occasionally, they'll pull over a Matatu or Bodaboda, leading to animated negotiations that seem to involve a lot of handshakes and discreet exchanges.

When rain joins the party, the drama intensifies. Hawkers scramble to cover their wares, passengers frantically roll up windows, and puddles form faster than you can say 'drainage system.' The jam grinds to a halt as drivers attempt to navigate flooded roads with the finesse of ship captains. Fares shoot up, tempers flare, and yet, somehow, life goes on.

Despite the chaos, there's something uniquely Kenyan about the traffic jam experience. It's a shared ordeal that fosters camaraderie and humor. After all, where else can you buy an umbrella, onions, pineapple, peanuts etc., catch a live argument, and get your side mirror fixed all without leaving your car?

The jam might delay you, frustrate you, and test your patience, but it also reminds you of the indomitable spirit of Kenyan life. Here, we don't just survive the jam, we thrive in it, turning every gridlock into an opportunity to hustle, laugh, and connect.

And when you finally reach your destination, hours later than planned, you'll find yourself with a story to tell because every Kenyan traffic jam is a chronicle, and every commuter is its author.

Chapter 4: Zebra Crossing? What's That?

If you're new to Kenya, you might notice the occasional white stripes painted across the road, otherwise known in theory as zebra crossings. They are meant to provide safe passage for pedestrians, emphasis on 'meant to.' In reality, a zebra crossing in Kenya is less of a sanctuary and more of a vague suggestion. Drivers see it as optional decoration, and pedestrians? Well, they see it as a challenge.

In Kenya, crossing the road isn't an act of transportation, it's an extreme sport. It requires timing, agility, and the unwavering belief that you can weave through a stream of speeding vehicles without a scratch. For pedestrians, every road is a potential crossing point. Why walk a few extra meters to a marked crossing when you can dart through traffic right where you stand? It's this fearless ingenuity that has earned Kenyan pedestrians the unofficial title of 'urban ninjas.'

The art of crossing begins with a look of steely determination. You step onto the road with a single goal: to get to the other side. Your tools? A raised hand, a quick side-eye at oncoming traffic, and, sometimes, a prayer. The raised hand is universal, it doesn't just signal cars to stop (they won't), but it also communicates, 'I'm going, and you better not hit me.' Drivers, in turn, will either honk aggressively or accelerate slightly as if testing your resolve.

Zebra crossings themselves are a study in irony. If you're lucky, you might find one with a faded sign promising pedestrians the right of way. But don't get too confident. Cars often barrel across these crossings as if the paint is invisible. On rare occasions, a good Samaritan will slow down and let you pass, but this is usually met with honks of protest from drivers behind them and mind you bodaboda won't be stopping when the car stops. It's a moment of brief respite wrapped in chaos.

But pedestrians are nothing if not adaptable. They've developed tactics to survive the madness. The 'Zigzag Shuffle' is a crowd favorite, where one weaves through moving cars with a mixture of hope and quick reflexes. Then there's the 'Power Walk Pause', a bold stride into the road, stopping mid, lane to let a vehicle pass, and resuming as if the interruption was part of the plan all along. Advanced pedestrians may attempt the 'Leap of Faith,' darting across a highway with the speed of a gazelle and the calm of a monk.

In coastal towns, the game takes on a different flavor. Here, pedestrians share the road with TukTuks and Bodabodas that dart unpredictably like mosquitoes in a dimly lit room. Add the scorching sun or a sudden rainstorm, and the crossings turn into a wet, slippery free-for-all where umbrellas double as shields and distractions.

The unsung heroes of this spectacle are the street kids and hawkers, who navigate traffic with the grace of seasoned pros. They'll cross roads balancing stacks of snacks on their heads, weaving through Matatus and trailers without so much as a glance back. It's equal parts awe-inspiring and nerve, wrecking.

And yet, despite the apparent chaos, there's an unspoken rhythm to it all. Pedestrians and drivers have a strange, almost telepathic understanding of each other. Cars will slow just enough to let someone squeeze through, and pedestrians will pause just enough to let a speeding Matatu whizz by. It's a delicate dance, performed daily on Kenya's roads, and remarkably, it works most of the time.

Of course, when something does go wrong, it's rarely subtle. A loud thud, a flurry of shouts, and suddenly the whole street is involved. Passersby rush in, opinions are shouted, and, within minutes, a full-blown trial unfolds on the tarmac. The driver and pedestrian will each have their defense teams (composed of random onlookers), and judgment is swift, if not entirely fair.

For outsiders, this might seem like chaos. But for Kenyans, it's just life. Crossing a road here isn't just about getting from point A to point B, it's about asserting your place in a system where survival depends on quick thinking, bold moves, and an occasional dash of luck.

So, the next time you approach a zebra crossing in Kenya, don't expect a driver to slow down or a pedestrian to wait. Instead, marvel at the intricate ballet of humanity and machinery, and remember: here, the rules of the road are less about paint and more about perseverance.

Chapter 5: Matatu DJs and Their Greatest Hits

Step into a Kenyan Matatu, and you're not just boarding a vehicle, you're entering a mobile entertainment hub. These minibuses are the lifeblood of Kenyan transport, but they're also a cultural phenomenon, offering a soundtrack to the chaos of the roads. Whether you're a fan of Afro beat, gospel, reggae, or 'that one song with too much bass and not enough lyrics,' Matatus have got you covered.

Matatu DJs are the unseen maestros of these rolling discos. They are the unsung heroes (or villains, depending on your mood) of Kenyan roads. These playlist wizards don't just pick songs; they curate experiences. And by 'experiences,' I mean they blast music loud enough to shake the fillings in your teeth and rattle the windows of passing cars. Subtlety is not in their vocabulary, but who needs subtlety when you have bass that can dislodge a traffic cone?

The playlist selection is an art form unto itself. Morning commuters are often greeted with gospel hits, a not so subtle attempt to cleanse their souls before tackling the day. Nothing like a spirited 'Yesu Ni Mwokozi' (Jesus is Savior) at full volume to remind you of the fragility of life especially when the Matatu driver is overtaking on a blind corner.

By midmorning, the playlist shifts. Enter reggae. Bob Marley classics and local reggae jams fill the air, giving off a 'chilled vibes' atmosphere that is in direct contrast to the chaos of the road. The irony of crooning 'One Love' while the driver honks aggressively at a hesitant pedestrian is not lost on anyone.

Afternoons belong to Afro beat and gengetone, the heartbeat of urban Kenya. These beats aren't just music; they're motivational anthems for survival. The bass reverberates so deeply you start to wonder if the Matatu's chassis is in danger of crumbling. Passengers nod along, partly to the rhythm and partly as a survival mechanism to blend in.

But the evenings? Oh, the evenings are where Matatu DJs truly shine. As the streets darken, the playlists take on a more eclectic flair. You'll get a random mix of RnB heartbreak anthems, nostalgic 90s jams, and, occasionally, a surprise Bollywood track. Why? Because Matatu DJs are artists, and artists are unpredictable.

Passengers are not just listeners, they're captive participants. Some enjoy the music, tapping their feet and humming along. Others endure it with the resigned expression of someone who didn't choose the soundtrack but is stuck with it anyway. Occasionally, someone will shout, 'Turn it down!' to no avail. The DJ's philosophy is simple: if you don't like the music, you can get off and walk. Don't think they will give you your fare back!

And then there are the sound systems. These are no ordinary speakers; they're industrial, grade sonic weapons. A fully equipped Matatu can have subwoofers under the seats, tweeters above the windows, and amplifiers powerful enough to drown out a passing jet. Sitting in the front seat means experiencing the music physically, you don't just hear it; you feel it in your bones.

For tourists, riding in a Matatu is an initiation. Many emerge from their first ride wide-eyed, clutching their bags, and muttering, 'That was... intense.' For Kenyans, though, it's just another day. The music, the chaos, the unsolicited DJ commentary, it's all part of the package.

And let's not forget the visual effects. Many Matatus come decked out in graffiti featuring global icons like Tupac, Messi, or, inexplicably, Barack Obama. These designs are as much a part of the experience as the music. A Matatu emblazoned with neon lights and a slogan like 'No Pain, No Gain' is not just a vehicle; it's a rolling statement piece.

Occasionally, you'll get a Matatu with a driver who fancies himself a DJ too. These are the riskiest rides, as the driver will spend as much time fiddling with the playlist as they do watching the road. It's a delicate balance, and passengers pray that the music selection doesn't come at the cost of their safety.

The humor and madness of Matatu music culture is a reflection of Kenya itself: vibrant, loud, unpredictable, and always moving to its own rhythm. So, the next time you find yourself on a Matatu, don't fight it. Let the music wash over you, nod along with the beat, and embrace the chaos. After all, life is better with a soundtrack, even if it's at full volume and slightly off-key.

Chapter 6: The Honk Symphony

In the great symphony of Kenyan roads, the car horn is both the conductor and the orchestra. It's not just a tool for warning or alerting; it's a universal language, a cultural cornerstone, and, occasionally, a weapon of mass irritation. The roads might be clogged, the rules might be bent beyond recognition, but one thing is certain: the honk always speaks.

To the untrained ear, a honk is just a noise, a sharp, intrusive interruption to an already chaotic soundscape. But in Kenya, a honk is layered with meaning, emotion, and intent. It's as versatile as a Swiss Army knife, used for everything from greetings to grievances. Short, sharp honks say, 'Move!' Long, drawn-out blasts declare, 'I'm not stopping, deal with it.' And then there's the rhythmic, almost musical honk, which says, 'Hey, I'm here, but I'm cool about it.'

Nowhere is this honk symphony more alive than at the intersections 'guided' by traffic police. Ideally, traffic lights should manage these junctions, with their green, yellow, and red offering an impartial, logical solution to traffic flow. But in Kenya, traffic lights are often ignored, malfunctioning, or mysteriously decommissioned; probably out of sheer frustration. Enter the traffic police, clad in white hats and reflective vests, attempting to impose order on the chaos.

Theirs is a pointless task. Armed with whistles and hand signals, they step bravely into the fray, a lone figure in a sea of honking vehicles. Their gestures are dramatic, almost theatrical, but rarely effective. A wave meant to halt traffic in one direction is met with honks of defiance and cars inching forward as if to test their resolve. From the other direction, drivers seize the opportunity to push through, honking enthusiastically to assert their right of way.

The honks directed at traffic police are a special category. There's the impatient honk, which says, 'I don't care what you're doing, let me through.' The sarcastic honk, which implies, 'Really? You think that's helping?' And the collaborative honk, where several drivers join forces in a horn, blasting symphony to express their collective frustration.

Sometimes, the honks get so loud and persistent that the police officer loses patience. They blow their whistle furiously, gesturing with increasing vigor, as though sheer volume and arm flailing will magically part the traffic like Moses and the Red Sea. It doesn't. If anything, it makes the drivers honk louder, a not so subtle reminder that the roads have their own rules, and the horn is king.

Ironically, many of these chaotic intersections are equipped with traffic lights, those beacons of order and reason. But in Kenya, traffic lights are more decorative than functional. Drivers treat a red light as a suggestion, a yellow light as an encouragement to speed up, and a green light as a reason to honk at anyone hesitating for a millisecond.

When traffic lights do work, they're often overridden by traffic police, who seem to trust their instincts more than the machines. The result? A confusing overlap of signals where drivers must choose between obeying the light, the police, or their own sense of survival. Naturally, most choose option three.

Adding to this chaos are the hawkers who see every traffic jam as a golden business opportunity. Armed with everything from boiled eggs to car chargers, they weave between the cars, their voices rising above the honks like soloists in this mad orchestra. The honking becomes their background music as they negotiate with impatient drivers, occasionally retreating just in time to avoid a Bodaboda zipping through the narrowest of gaps.

In rare moments, the honking reaches a fever pitch and transforms into a form of protest. Drivers stuck in an interminable jam caused by a rogue pothole, a stalled truck, or sheer human stubbornness will unite in a chorus of frustration. The horns blare in unison, a deafening cry for justice or at least for the jam to clear.

But the real magic of the honk symphony is that, somehow, it works. Despite the chaos, the noise, and the seeming lack of order, Kenyan roads keep moving. People get where they're going, even if they arrive with frazzled nerves and a faint ringing in their ears. The honk isn't just a sound; it's the heartbeat of the roads, a chaotic yet strangely effective rhythm that keeps the country moving.

So, the next time you find yourself in the middle of a honk, fueled showdown, don't despair. Just sit back, listen, and appreciate the unintentional artistry of the honk symphony. It's not just traffic, it's a cultural experience.

Chapter 7: Bodaboda Uber, Your Ride, Your Risk

If you've never taken a ride on a Bodaboda in Kenya, you've missed out on an adrenaline, packed cultural phenomenon. Part transportation, part thrill ride, and part survival test, these motorcycle taxis are the kings of convenience, and chaos. Need to get somewhere in a hurry? A Bodaboda will weave through traffic like an action hero dodging explosions. Of course, whether you arrive with your nerves intact is another question entirely.

Some Bodabodas are official Ubers of Kenya, but with a twist, your ride comes with wind in your hair, a dash of danger, and, if you're lucky, a helmet that's seen better days. They promise speed and deliver it in spades, often making you wonder if they're racing an invisible clock.

Your typical Bodaboda rider has an unmatched confidence that can only come from years of dodging Matatus, potholes, and traffic police.

With the throttle wide open, they glide past gridlocked cars, squeeze into impossible gaps, and occasionally mount sidewalks when the road refuses to cooperate. It's like they're starring in their own action movie, only the explosions are replaced by pedestrians scattering for dear life.

The Bodaboda experience begins with the helmet. By law, every rider is required to provide a helmet for the passenger. In reality, this often means a faded, cracked piece of plastic that looks more decorative than functional. And if you're unlucky to get one, you end up sharing one with the last ten passengers sweaty, fragrant evidence included.

For those bold enough to ride helmetless, the risk is offset by a curious mix of faith and fatalism. 'If it's my time, it's my time,' a rider might say with a shrug, before roaring off into oncoming traffic. You, the passenger, are left clutching their jacket and hoping it's not your time just yet.

Bodaboda riders approach traffic laws with the same enthusiasm a cat approaches water, minimal and begrudging. Red light? That's a suggestion. Zebra crossing? A slalom course. One-way street? Merely a mild inconvenience. The road belongs to those brave enough to claim it, and Bodabodas are nothing if not bold.

This disregard for the rules is matched only by their creativity in evading traffic police. Spotting a checkpoint ahead, your rider will execute a sharp U-turn, zip down a side street, or even disappear into a maize field. 'Don't worry, we'll take a shortcut,' they'll say, as you cling to the bike and wonder if shortcuts always involve livestock and muddy footpaths. At times, they will just go through the check point in some cat and mouse game.

Before you even hop on, there's the small matter of negotiating the fare. Bodaboda riders are master hagglers, and every ride begins with a spirited debate over the price. 'Two hundred? That's robbery!' you'll exclaim. 'Fuel prices have gone up!' they'll retort, as though the global economy is directly tied to your five-minute trip to the market. Eventually, you'll settle on a fee somewhere between daylight robbery and outright charity.

Of course, the fare is only half the story. There's also the matter of your cargo. Bodabodas are infamous for their ability to transport the unimaginable. Furniture? No problem. A sack of potatoes? Easy. A family of three plus a goat? Challenge accepted. Watching a Bodaboda laden with precariously balanced goods is both terrifying and awe-inspiring.

Every Bodaboda ride is an adventure. There's the thrill of speed as you zip past cars stuck in traffic, the jarring reality check when you hit a pothole, and the surreal conversations with your rider. 'You know, this bike can outrun a car,' they'll boast, as the engine sputters on a steep hill.

Then there are the spills, thankfully, most are minor. A sudden brake to avoid a pedestrian, a skid on a muddy road, or an overly ambitious attempt to climb a curb. If you're lucky, you'll walk away with nothing more than a story to tell.

And oh, the stories! Like the time your rider stopped mid ride to buy miraa (a local stimulant), promising it would 'make the ride faster.' Or when you found yourself in the middle of a Bodaboda rally, a spontaneous race that turned a quiet road into a scene from Mad Max.

Love them or fear them, Bodabodas are an integral part of Kenyan life. They're the unsung heroes of the roads, braving traffic jams, rainstorms, and potholes to get you where you need to go. Sure, the ride might leave you breathless, disheveled, and questioning your life choices, but you'll also arrive with a newfound appreciation for their daring spirit.

So, the next time you're late for a meeting or stuck in Nairobi traffic, consider hopping on a Bodaboda. It might just be the fastest, most thrilling, and utterly unforgettable ride of your life. Just don't forget to negotiate the fare and say a quick prayer before you hop on.

CHAPTER 8: THE CART Chaos

If there's one mode of transport in Kenya that can single-handedly slow down an entire lane of traffic while defying every known rule of the road, it's the humble cart. These hand, pulled or donkey, pulled vehicles, colloquially referred to as "Mkokoteni", are an indispensable part of Kenya's bustling trade ecosystem. Yet, for many road users, they are a source of endless frustration.

Early morning on the chaotic streets of Nairobi while people are trying to go to work or to their hustles, a cart piled high with fruits, vegetables, or even bales of secondhand clothes from the Wakulima Market or the famous Gikomba Market. These carts, often overloaded with unimaginable weight, move at a glacial pace. Their operators, usually a single individual or a pair pulling with all their might, are oblivious to the traffic building up behind them. On a steep incline, their struggle becomes a spectacle, straining bodies, immobile carts, and an orchestra of impatient car horns echoing in the air.

To make matters worse, these carts often face the wrong direction on the road, creating a maddening mix of chaos and danger. In the dim light of early dawn, spotting a Mkokoteni on a busy highway can feel like playing a high, stakes game of dodgeball. With no reflective strips, no lights, and often no visible sign of the person pulling it, a collision feels almost inevitable. And if you think they'll move aside to let vehicles pass, think again. Cart pullers are notoriously stubborn and will maintain their slow and steady pace, no matter how many drivers they inconvenience. Their sense of road etiquette? Nonexistent.

The problem isn't limited to urban areas, either. On highways and dual carriageways, these carts creep along, creating dangerous situations as vehicles swerve to avoid them. Uphill roads are particularly infamous for cart jams, where overloaded carts grind to a halt, holding up entire lanes of traffic as frustrated drivers fume in their vehicles. Any attempt to reason with the cart pullers is usually met with arrogance or outright indifference, leaving road users feeling powerless.

The most baffling part? Despite their critical role in Kenya's economy, Mkokoteni operators seem blissfully unaware of road signs, highway codes, or even the basic flow of traffic. They'll pull their carts onto any road they choose, be it a bustling highway or a narrow market alley, with no regard for the chaos they leave in their wake. They're not just oblivious, they're unshakably confident in their right to be there. The tragedy is that the traffic police pretend not to see them and if they do, there is little they can do.

Carts are a paradox on Kenyan roads. On one hand, they are a lifeline for traders and an essential cog in the wheel of commerce, ferrying goods where motorized vehicles often cannot go. On the other hand, their slow speeds, massive loads, and road oblivion make them a menace to modern traffic systems. As much as they are admired for their utility, they are equally loathed for the bottlenecks and headaches they cause.

In Kenya, the cart chaos is just another part of the unpredictable road landscape, a mix of necessity, defiance, and sheer inconvenience. Whether you admire their resilience or curse their presence, one thing is certain: they have been here too long, they're not going anywhere, and neither are you if you get stuck behind one.

Chapter 9: Truck Trouble

Trucks are the unsung giants of Kenya's roads, moving everything from fresh water to massive boulders across the country. But these behemoths often turn into rolling obstacles, especially when they encounter hilly terrain. The experience of driving behind one can range from mildly frustrating to downright terrifying.

Water trucks, an essential lifeline in water, scarce areas, bring relief to many, but their journey is often fraught with unintended comedy and chaos. As they ascend steep hills, with example being Kingara road for the trucks bringing water from Ngong road; water begins to slosh out from poorly secured tanks, creating mini rivers on the road. Not only does this waste precious cargo, but the sudden water flow also leaves slippery patches on the tarmac, making overtaking a risky gamble. Drivers trailing behind these trucks find themselves dodging puddles and hoping their tires don't lose grip on the makeshift wet road.

The stone carriers are another sinful feature on Kenyan roads. If there's one type of truck to avoid at all costs, it's the stone carriers. These trucks, often loaded with massive rocks or construction materials, are a gamble on hills. As they crawl upwards, their overworked engines groan, and the trucks can start rolling backward without warning. A lack of proper maintenance means their brakes may fail or simply give out under the load, turning the truck into a deadly boulder on wheels.

One of the most dangerous places where you'll encounter these treacherous trucks is the infamous escarpment road towards Mai Mahiu. This winding route, cutting through the Rift Valley, is a major highway for tourists heading to the world-renowned Masai Mara. The steep inclines and sharp bends make it a nightmare for any driver, but for stone carriers, it's a ticking time bomb. Whether they're struggling uphill or barreling downhill, the threat they pose is constant. The weight of their cargo, combined with poor maintenance and overloaded frames, often results in unpredictable movements. Being anywhere near these trucks, especially on such challenging terrain, is courting disaster.

Even when they manage to stay put, many of these trucks lack functioning brake lights or hazard signals. On a dark, steep road, an unlit stationary truck becomes a death trap, especially for unsuspecting drivers barreling around corners at night. It's a moment of sheer panic when a driver suddenly realizes the massive silhouette ahead isn't moving.

Kenyan trucks are infamous for their oblivion to lane discipline. Whether it's a single, lane highway or a multi-lane road, these trucks often claim whatever lane they fancy, regardless of traffic flow. On dual carriageways, it's not uncommon to find two trucks side by side in the inside lanes, holding up miles of traffic as they compete in a slow-motion race to the summit of a hill. Frustrated drivers honk, flash lights, and wave frantically, but the truckers are unfazed, cruising at their own pace and disregarding the chaos behind them.

One of the most dangerous habits of Kenyan truck drivers is their tendency to stop abruptly on hills. Without proper signals or warning lights, these unplanned halts become catastrophic traps for anyone following too closely. Add to this the unpredictable loads like unsecured stones, bags of charcoal, or towering stacks of sugarcane and you have a recipe for disaster. A sudden stop can send cargo tumbling onto the road or, worse, onto other vehicles.

Trucks in Kenya seem to operate in their own parallel universe when it comes to understanding lanes. The concept of fast lanes and slow lanes is completely foreign to many drivers. Even on steep inclines, where slow, moving vehicles are expected to stick to the outermost lane, trucks will unapologetically cruise in the middle or fast lane, effectively creating a roadblock for everyone else. Drivers stuck behind these moving barricades are left fuming as the line of vehicles grows longer with each passing second.

Driving near trucks at night adds another layer of danger. With missing or dimly lit tail lights, these massive vehicles are almost invisible until it's too late. The trucks that ferry goods during the night often lack proper reflectors, turning them into camouflaged obstacles against the dark backdrop of Kenyan highways. Overtaking one becomes a nerve, wrecking gamble, especially on unlit roads with sharp curves.

Despite the hazards, trucks are a necessary evil on Kenyan roads. They bring water to drought, stricken towns, transport vital construction materials, and keep the wheels of commerce turning. But their erratic behavior, water spills, sudden stops, lane hogging, and backward rolling makes them a source of anxiety for every motorist.

Kenyan roads are a battleground of patience and survival, and trucks are the unpredictable giants in this chaotic mix. Whether you're dodging splashes from a water truck, praying a stone carrier doesn't roll back, or stuck behind two trucks hogging lanes, the only guarantee is that you'll have a story to tell by the end of your journey.

Chapter 10: Pothole Pioneers

If you've ever driven or even strolled along a Kenyan road, chances are you've had a memorable encounter with potholes. These craters aren't mere nuisances; they're like unwelcome, persistent companions that show up when you least expect them. Just when you think you've managed to avoid them, there they are ready to send your car swerving, your tires groaning in protest. And let's not underestimate their depth. Some potholes are so cavernous you'd think they were carved for a canoe, with enough room left over for a picnic basket. Throw in a splash of rain or a trickle of sewer water, and they morph into miniature lakes, turning every journey into an unpredictable adventure.

Now, you might ask, 'Wait a minute, aren't we paying road taxes?' Yes, we are. And yes, the potholes persist. The question we're all secretly wondering is: What exactly are we paying for? If the roads are being maintained if the taxes are doing something, then why does it feel like we're traversing a post, apocalyptic landscape? This is a developing country with many roads with more craters than the moon, footpaths that double as hawker stalls, and an overall infrastructure that seems to have been designed by someone with a distinct love for chaos.

These potholes are more than just annoyances; they're part of the Kenyan driving experience, like an obstacle course that you didn't sign up for. You're cruising along the highway, nodding to your favorite song, when out of nowhere, the road disappears. Well, not literally but it might as well have. You hit a pothole that feels like you've gone off-roading in an SUV, and you're in a Toyota Corolla. It's an art form, this pothole dodging. You'll swerve left, veer right, then counter, steer to avoid the next one, all the while pretending you're not about to face, plant into a traffic jam because you've just gone off-track for the third time in five minutes.

But it doesn't stop there. Some of these potholes are so generously sized that they don't just challenge your driving skills, they challenge your sanity. It's like driving on a road map designed by someone who was told to 'make it as difficult as possible.' And the best part? Even when they finally get filled (after what seems like an eternity), they only last until the next mild rainstorm. Why bother paving them properly when we can have a perpetual pothole party, right?

And let's talk about pedestrian footpaths or more accurately, the idea of footpaths. In theory, roads should have clearly marked footpaths for pedestrians, because let's face it, not everyone is driving (or, in some cases, even walking on the road). But in reality, what we have is a beautiful mishmash of things that don't quite qualify as proper footpaths.

You're walking down the street, hoping to reach your destination without having to dodge oncoming vehicles, when you realize the footpath has transformed into a hawker's market. One moment, you're trying to navigate around a pile of secondhand shoes; the next, you're stepping over piles of bananas. And just when you think you've mastered the art of sidestepping vendors, you encounter a deep hole, a real one, not just metaphorical. These aren't the cute little puddles you can jump over; these are craters.

You look up and realize there's an electrical wire hanging dangerously low, threatening to turn this already hazardous walk into a potential electrocution experience. And it gets worse. You realize this isn't just happening in one corner of the city. This is the norm. No footpaths, random stalls, dangling wires, and massive potholes.

And then, the pièce de résistance, the drainage system, or should I say, lack thereof. You'd think with all the road taxes collected, a few basic amenities might be installed. Perhaps some gutters to carry away rainwater? But no. In Kenya, the drainage system is often an afterthought, a conceptual design that only appears in government documents but never on the streets. When it rains, the roads become rivers, and pedestrians must navigate puddles that have more in common with swamps than sidewalks. Those brave enough to walk the streets during heavy rains find themselves ankle, deep in water, dodging random debris, hoping they don't step into a deep hole that's cleverly disguised as a puddle. Most of the times this water is a mix of sewer water and rain water.

We pay road taxes, we hear about planned drainage projects, but the reality is that we're still waiting for some rainwater management that doesn't involve the streets becoming temporary lakes.

On top of that, there's the incredible proliferation of hawkers. They aren't just selling fruits and vegetables or trinkets, they've practically built empires. They've claimed every available inch of the footpath, making the roads more of a shared experience between pedestrians and vendors than anything else. Some streets have entire demolished houses on the side of the road. You're trying to make your way from one side of the street to the other, but you can't because there's a stall blocking your path. Move one inch to the left, and boom, there's a basket of tomatoes. Shift right, and suddenly, there's a bundle of plastic chairs.

They truly are ingenious. The way they've transformed those humble footpaths into bustling mini malls is nothing short of remarkable. You can find everything from electronics and household goods to clothing and, if luck is on your side, even a dog, a goat or two. But just when you think you've successfully navigated the maze of vendors, you're greeted by a mountain of discarded plastic bags and rubbish. It's ironic, considering Kenya proudly banned single, use plastic bags, yet here lies a stark reminder of the uphill battle against waste.

At some point, you start asking the big questions. Is this what road taxes are funding? Is this the best we can do with all the money we pay? The potholes are deep, the pedestrian lanes are more like obstacle courses, and the streets are a marketplace, a construction site, and a trash heap all rolled into one. How is this normal?

Where are the funds going? Where are the urban planners? Why hasn't something changed after all these years? It's a rhetorical question we all ask, hoping the answer might arrive on the next rainstorm or the next 'road improvement project' that never seems to be finished.

And yet, despite the chaos, the traffic, the lack of infrastructure, and the ever, present hazard of stepping into a puddle that might just swallow you whole, we keep driving, walking, and surviving. Kenyan roads are a testament to the resilience of its people; the pothole pioneers who navigate each day with the same unfazed attitude. It's not pretty, it's not ideal, but somehow, it works. And as the saying goes, 'What doesn't kill you... just might give you a broken axle or a sprained ankle.' But we carry on, undeterred, with our helmets, our pothole, dodging skills, and our unwavering belief that one day, just one day, we'll have roads that are worthy of the taxes we pay.

Chapter 11: The Highway Hustlers'

Kenyan roads are more than just thoroughfares, they're the heartbeat of a thriving roadside economy, and nowhere is this more evident than in the traffic jams. When the car comes to a halt, the real business begins. It's a bizarre, entrepreneurial wonderland, where hawkers and vendors are the true kings and queens of the road. Forget about the formal economy, this is where the hustle thrives.

But there is one road that remains immune to this chaotic economy: The Expressway. The road that connects Jomo Kenyatta International Airport (JKIA) to the James Gichuru intersection. The one that's a toll road. It's the only road in Kenya where you can drive without the threat of your car being surrounded by hawkers trying to sell you everything from snacks to live goats. The Expressway stands as a shining beacon of what could be, a vision of a future where roads are actually... well, roads, not bustling marketplaces. It's a paid toll road, which, though a financial burden, does give you one benefit: no hustlers. Yes, the expressway is blessedly free from the chaotic hustle of Kenyan road commerce.

So let's explore the madness of the rest of the roads; the roads where hustling is not just a way of life but a form of art. These hustlers are always on the lookout for a trapped audience, someone stuck in traffic. Whether you're stuck in jam for ten minutes or two hours, it doesn't matter; these enterprising souls are here to make a sale.

First up, the snack vendors. These are the OG hustlers. They operate at a level of efficiency that should honestly be studied in business schools. You haven't truly lived until you've witnessed a snack vendor zigzagging between moving cars, all while balancing a tray of roasted maize, peanuts, or mandazis on their head like some sort of high, stakes circus performer.

You'll find them in every major traffic jam, darting between cars with the precision of a pro athlete. Their sales pitches are short and sweet, shouted with the kind of enthusiasm that makes you feel guilty for not buying something. 'Mandazi, hot and fresh! Only 20 bob!' they shout, like they're offering the last slice of pizza on earth. It's amazing how quickly the car windows roll down, as if a collective hunger for hot snacks has suddenly overtaken everyone.

And then, as if on cue, another hustler appears on the other side, offering roasted maize, steaming in the sweltering heat. The maize vendors are especially crafty grilled to perfection and just spicy enough to make you question your decision to buy something off the street, but too good to pass up. Again the escarpment road going to Mai Mahiu is one of the places to find these maize vendors. And don't forget the fruit vendors, those who bring pineapple, mango, Apples and watermelon, which is a refreshing break when you're stuck in traffic on a hot day. The sheer volume of snacks sold in these jams could feed an entire city if there was a more reliable way of distributing food. But as it is, the bustling highway food market is one of the most important informal sectors in the country.

But why stop at snacks when you can sell a live goat? The highway hustlers are nothing if not resourceful. Amid the blaring horns and seething frustration of gridlock, a man with a goat on a leash appears on the side of the road especially holiday time, Christmas is the mother of all. And just like that, a conversation ensues about the merits of that particular goat. It's astounding how, in the midst of a traffic jam, people can negotiate the price of a goat as though they're deciding what vegetables to buy in the market. You'll have one guy telling you how the goat is perfect for a wedding, while another insists that it's the best meat' for a Christmas celebration. There's always that one guy who's ready to sell you a chicken, and you don't even remember how he got into your lane. The creativity of these hustlers is something to behold.

And yes, this is all part of the charm of the Kenyan highway economy. Because when you're stuck in traffic, your car becomes a marketplace, and every vendor has something to offer, whether it's food, drink, or even the occasional live animal. You'd think these spontaneous vendors could sell anything. 'Looking for a speaker? I've got one.' 'What about a mirror? Here you go.' It's not unusual to find people selling everything from fresh fruit to electronics, with a sales pitch that could convince you to buy something you don't even need.

But the hustlers don't stop at food and animals, they've got it all covered. Ever had the inexplicable desire to buy a secondhand phone case while stuck in a jam? Well, someone on the roadside is ready to fulfill that wish. The same goes for watches, sunglasses, and the occasional dubious 'genuine' perfume. If the hustle is real, then these vendors are making it even more real. You'd be surprised by how many items can be sold within a single traffic jam. There are also the small, time repair guys who are ready to patch up a punctured tire, fix a broken side mirror, or even clean your windshield while you wait for the traffic lights to finally turn green.

It's like a mobile shopping mall that exists only in the most frustrating moments of your day. The hustle never ends whether it's delivering something you didn't ask for or simply giving you an opportunity to leave with more things than you expected to buy. There's always something to be sold, and if you're not buying, you're definitely being offered something. Maybe next time it'll be that bright red saucepan or a set of speaker wires.

The hustlers have an unspoken code; adapt and survive. The weather may be scorching hot or pouring rain, but you'll find them out there, navigating between cars with ease, knowing that there's an opportunity to make a sale if they're fast enough. And if the traffic isn't moving, that's even better. The longer the jam, the more items get sold. It's like a game of patience and strategy. There's a deep level of understanding between the vendors and the drivers too; a look from a driver means a sale might happen, while a flash of impatience could mean the vendor will simply move on. It's a subtle dance, and the hustlers know how to keep the rhythm going.

In all this chaos, it's easy to forget one simple fact: The Expressway. The only road where you're free from the mad scramble of traffic jam sales. When you're on the Expressway, you can actually focus on driving and enjoying the smooth ride, uninterrupted by people selling goats or charging your phone. It's a luxury, really, one that costs a toll to enjoy. And that's the great irony paying for the peace and quiet of a traffic jam, free zone. Shame it's not long enough, by the time you get to James Gichuru intersection or Mlolongo that peace and smooth ride is gone.

All this hustle, while chaotic, is undeniably a reflection of the country's ingenuity and drive. Kenya has one of the most vibrant informal economies in the world, and the hustle that takes place on its roads is a living, breathing testament to the entrepreneurial spirit of its people. Whether it's food, fashion, or farm animals, the hustle never stops. For every traffic jam that traps you, there's someone out there trying to make a sale. And the best part? They often succeed.

So, next time you're stuck in a jam, surrounded by a sea of hawkers offering you everything under the sun, take a moment to appreciate the ingenuity behind it all. After all, the hustle isn't just a way of life, it's the backbone of Kenya's economy, the roadside lifeblood that keeps everything moving... even if it's just a goat, a bag of mandazis, and a fresh melon being passed through your car window.

Chapter 12: The Seatbelt Saga

Ah, seatbelts, the supposed safety feature that every vehicle in Kenya should be equipped with. The law says that every passenger in a public vehicle is supposed to wear a seatbelt. It's a simple rule, really. One that's meant to protect your life in the event of an emergency. Yet, when it comes to Matatus, the idea of seatbelts as anything more than decorative embellishments is almost laughable.

Once upon a time, a tough Minister named Michuki introduced stringent laws that made sure every Matatu had working seatbelts, and passengers actually used them. For a brief moment in history, safety felt achievable on Kenyan roads. But after Michuki's untimely death, enforcement fizzled out, and things quickly went back to the usual chaos.

Nowadays, seatbelts in Matatus are more like relics of that era, dangling loosely or sometimes nonexistent altogether. When they are present, they're often in such a sorry state that passengers would rather take their chances without them. Dirty and tattered, the belts might not even buckle, with some buckles jammed, rusted, or missing entirely. If you do manage to fasten one, you might find it suspiciously short and uncomfortable or laughably loose, doing nothing more than reminding you that safety is mostly wishful thinking. It's as if they're there to check a box rather than actually save lives.

And heaven forbid you actually get a seatbelt that works! Because what happens when you fasten it? You've just committed a cardinal sin in the world of Matatu transport: you've slowed the driver down. The whole point of a Matatu is speed, and if a seatbelt is going to get in the way of that, it's just not part of the plan. Most of the time, you'll find yourself contemplating whether you should ask the driver if they can drive a little faster so that you can arrive at your destination before your seatbelt is needed. But no one does, because we all know that the real question is not 'Are we safe?' but rather, 'Are we getting there faster than the guy in the next lane?'

The truth is that Matatus, while equipped with seatbelts in theory, operate on a different set of laws, ones that have nothing to do with safety and everything to do with survival and speed. These vehicles are essentially mini racetracks on wheels. The driver, determined to get you from point A to point B in record time, will often ignore the seatbelt issue altogether. In fact, in most Matatus, the seatbelts are treated like abstract concepts, a mere suggestion by those bureaucrats in Nairobi who seem to think safety is something to be taken seriously. But seriously, who has time for that when you're trying to keep up with the insane pace of Matatu racing?

Now, as if the seatbelt saga wasn't chaotic enough, enter the Bodaboda. If you think Matatus are a wild ride, wait until you hop on one of these two, wheeled daredevils. Riding a Bodaboda isn't about seatbelts; it's about balance, grip, and sheer nerve. The concept of a safety harness here is laughable. The 'passenger' on a Bodaboda doesn't even have the luxury of holding onto the seat in front of them; they have to cling onto the rider and or other passengers for dear life as they weave through traffic like they're auditioning for an action movie stunt.

It's not unusual to see three or four people precariously balancing on a single Bodaboda, as if the traffic laws were written for someone else entirely. And if you're lucky, the driver might even have a helmet; most of the time, though, you'll have to fight the wind and pray you're not knocked off while dodging potholes, pedestrians, and other daredevils.

You'd think that after all these years, there would be some sort of enforcement. But no, in Kenya, law enforcement tends to take a backseat to the realities of public transport life. There's an entire law about seatbelts in public vehicles, but no one really cares. The Matatu drivers know it, the passengers know it, and the police know it. The truth is that the drivers who own and operate these Matatus understand one thing: safety doesn't sell. Speed does.

So what does that mean for the average commuter? You've got two choices: ride fast or ride faster. Either way, your life is in the hands of the gods and the drivers. Just make sure you're buckling your seatbelt if there is any, not because you think it will save you, but because it's the only semblance of order you're going to get. Besides, there's a certain comfort in knowing that even though the seatbelt may not be saving you, at least you're contributing to the illusion of safety, which is kind of like being in an action movie, except the stakes are a lot higher and the special effects are far less convincing.

Let's not even talk about the other horrors of safety regulations that are completely ignored in Matatus. In a world where seatbelts are optional, window bars are sometimes a welcome feature. At least they provide a bit of protection from the outside world or, in some cases, from the inside. You never know when a fight will break out between passengers over the right to change the music. There's nothing more entertaining than seeing a commuter with no seatbelt get catapulted from one end of the van to the other as a result of a hard swerve while trying to avoid a Bodaboda that's just squeezed through a gap that should never have existed.

But then, this isn't about safety. It's about survival. The real question isn't whether or not you're buckled up. It's whether or not you make it to your destination without being caught in one of the countless hazards of urban traffic. After all, in the world of Matatus, the ride is never guaranteed to be smooth seatbelts or not.

In summary, the Seatbelt Saga is a daily reality for anyone who rides in public vehicles in Kenya. It's a never-ending dance between the law and the will of the people, where safety and speed are constantly at odds, and the laws are seen as mere suggestions. It's a reminder that, while there are rules in place, the road to Kenyan transport often leads to a very different place.

Chapter 13: Reverse is a Gear Too

In Kenya, driving is a fluid experience one where the rules seem to bend, twist, and stretch to accommodate the unique ways of getting from point A to point B. And nowhere is this more apparent than in the art of 'reverse parking' or, as it's known in some circles, 'just reversing to make your way.' The philosophy is simple: why bother going forward when reversing works just as well?

Let's start with the highways, those grand roads meant to facilitate long, distance travel and smooth, uninterrupted journeys. Here, you'll often find that the concept of 'one way' is more of a guideline than a rule. Imagine driving on the Nairobi, Mombasa highway. You're cruising along at a comfortable speed, humming to the latest Matatu hits on the radio, when suddenly, bam you see a car coming straight toward you. Not a head, on collision scenario, mind you. No, no. This car is doing the opposite of what it should. It's reversing. And it's doing so with the same confidence as someone driving forward, except this time, they've decided that reversing is far more efficient when you have missed a junction.

In some instances, the road is wide enough to allow this reverse maneuver. The car, in all its audacity, veers onto the shoulder and begins to slowly but surely reverse down the highway. At first, it's slow, almost imperceptible, as if the driver is waiting for divine intervention. But no, the car picks up speed, navigating the rough shoulder with the skill of a tractor driver in a field of potholes. And you're left sitting there, utterly confused, wondering if you should follow suit. After all, why go forward when reversing seems to work so well for this bold pioneer?

And this isn't limited to the highways alone. No, no, no. The art of reversing to your destination is also commonly practiced at intersections and side roads. Most drivers would simply yield or wait for a safe moment to join the main road. But not in Kenya. Here, the side road driver doesn't just pull onto the main road, oh no, they reverse. They reverse in such a way that you start to question if this is a new traffic law you're unaware of. It's as if they've decided that the idea of merging into traffic is overrated, so instead, they just reverse onto the main road with all the gusto of a race car driver in a demolition derby.

This reverse into traffic maneuver isn't just confined to one or two brave souls. No, it's a nationwide tradition. Whether you're on a busy highway or a quiet backstreet, someone, somewhere, is about to break out the reverse gear and use it as their weapon of choice. The moment they start their reverse journey, everything changes. You, the unsuspecting driver, suddenly become part of an impromptu game of dodge the reverse. It's a dance, a test of reflexes, patience, and, frankly, the ability to make quick decisions. Will they stop? Will they keep going? And, most importantly, will they ever realize that reverse isn't the best way forward?

But perhaps the most hilariously dangerous reversal happens when someone decides that backing up into traffic is a perfectly valid way to 'merge.' Yes, this is where the real magic happens. The traffic lights are out, naturally, and chaos reigns as everyone tries to go in every direction at once. You've been waiting at the light, fingers tapping anxiously on your steering wheel, when a car pulls up behind you. It's too far from the curb to be making a right turn, so what do they do? They put their hazards on and reverse, not slowly, like you'd expect. No, they reverse with the intent of getting around you. And just like that, you're stuck, literally.

You now have two options: panic or watch in awe as this reverse, genius executes a perfect twirl around your car and into traffic. If you happen to be in the front seat of the vehicle behind, good luck. There's no room for fear in this high, stakes game. You'll either get out and let them finish their work or close your eyes and pray they don't ram into you in their bid to outmaneuver the system. Either way, you're in for a front, row seat to a traffic dance performance that would make even the most seasoned drivers shake their heads.

The truth is, reversing is not just a gear, it's a philosophy. And it's not just confined to the small roads or residential areas. It's practiced everywhere. Highways, backstreets, and even parking lots. The fact that there are rules about 'going forward' on the road seems like a distant memory to anyone who's spent more than five minutes in traffic. Reversing, it turns out, is the preferred method of transportation when all else fails. Need to get out of a jam? Reverse. Need to break the monotony of a slow, moving line of cars? Reverse. Want to get to the front of the line at a stop sign? Reverse.

And why is this so effective, you ask? Because Kenya. In a country where creativity is prized above all else, the reverse gear is the epitome of ingenious problem, solving. There's no need to follow the rules when you can bend them to your will. In fact, it's often the best way to get things done. The other drivers? They'll just have to deal with it. After all, it's not just a gear; it's a strategy.

In the end, what is the purpose of going forward when reversing feels like the only sensible option? When in doubt, hit that reverse gear and show the world what you're really made of. After all, in Kenya, reverse is a gear too, and it's a gear that gets you exactly where you want to be eventually.

Chapter 14: The Overload Olympics

Overloading has become an unfortunate reality for nearly every vehicle on Kenyan roads. Whether it's cars, buses, lorries, bodabodas, or even carts, the practice of pushing vehicles beyond their capacity has become alarmingly common. What should be a simple act of transportation often turns into a dangerous game of "how much can we load?" The line between what's safe and what's recklessly excessive has been blurred, with overloaded vehicles not only risking breakdowns but, more seriously, jeopardizing lives.

From packed buses swaying under the weight of passengers to bodabodas carrying unimaginable loads, the sheer scale of overloading is a clear indication of how little regard there is for safety on the roads. This is no longer just a matter of inconvenience; it's a deadly reality that continues to endanger lives daily. The weight limits that should govern vehicle capacities are largely ignored, replaced by a mentality that views them as mere suggestions, putting everyone at risk in the process.

It starts with the Matatu, the beloved minibuses that serve as the pulse of Kenya's public transport system. Now, let's get this clear: the advertised seating capacity? It's just a number. A rough estimate. A hopeful suggestion. Because in reality, a Matatu can and will carry far more than any sane person would ever attempt. How many people can you fit into a Matatu? The answer: as many as you can possibly cram in, and then some.

You've got your standard load: passengers sitting shoulder to shoulder, their legs expertly intertwined with the legs of their neighbors. But then, you'll witness the spectacle of Matatu 'Tetris', a phenomenon where even the air inside the bus gets filled to capacity. Passengers sit, stand and even crouch in impossible ways, all while the driver accelerates with the confidence of someone whose vehicle is impervious to the laws of physics. And if you think that's wild, just wait until you see the extra cargo.

Oh yes, Matatus are not just for people. Need to transport a sack of potatoes? No problem, there's always room for more spuds in the aisles. Oh, there's always space for anything in these Matatus. The Matatu conductors have mastered the delicate art of packing passengers like an expert. With years of practice, they can fit in just one more person, no matter how cramped the space. "Sawa, sawa! There's space, just squeeze in!" they shout, as they expertly navigate the overcrowded Matatu, expertly balancing bodies like a seasoned professional. Their skill in packing people in is a qualification of its own, ensuring that not a single inch of space goes unused, often pushing the limits of what seems physically possible.

But it's not just Matatus that are redefining the very concept of load, bearing. The Bodaboda, the motorcycle taxis that brave everything from potholes to erratic drivers, are also champions in the Overload Olympics. You've seen them, right? You know, the Bodaboda that has somehow managed to transform from a simple means of transport into a rolling cargo ship. Think four passengers, yes, four crammed onto a motorcycle that was clearly designed for one. The driver's knees are pinned to his chest, but that's the price of friendship in Kenya. The other passengers? They're balanced like circus performers, holding on to whatever they can, sometimes each other, sometimes the air itself, but always somehow managing not to fall off.

And if you think this is an isolated case, think again. Bodabodas regularly carry loads that defy all logic and safety standards; sacks of potatoes, multiple crates of eggs, or even four gas cylinders, all precariously balanced as the driver weaves through traffic at high speed. Safety is often disregarded in favor of speed and efficiency, as the focus is solely on getting the job done, no matter the risk. The lack of concern for comfort or proper loading highlights a serious disregard for both personal and public safety, with little regard for the consequences.

And then, of course, we have the TukTuk, those little three, wheeled marvels that ply the coastal towns and urban areas with equal zest. A TukTuk's primary purpose is clear: transport people from point A to point B without much fanfare. But what happens when there's a shortage of room? Well, the rules get a bit... flexible. Need to transport a small family of five? No problem. The TukTuk can handle that, if you sit two people in the front seat, three on the back seat. It's not pretty, but it works. Need to ferry some chairs or three sacks of maize flour? You'd be surprised at how much can be stuffed into the tiny confines of a TukTuk. The only limiting factor? The driver's courage.

It's a spectacle that never fails to amuse or baffle. The drivers, with a casual wave, zip through traffic with a cargo load that would make a lorry driver sweat. And while the passengers may not be exactly comfortable, they're certainly going to get where they're going, and at a speed that would make a Formula 1 driver envious. It's all part of the fun, isn't it?

Let's not overlook the trucks, the lorries of Kenya, often the epitome of overload. These vehicles are so heavily loaded that the road itself could file a complaint. Whether it's transporting massive amounts of household goods, construction materials, or even livestock, the lorries often carry loads so high that they seem to defy the laws of physics. The cargo is stacked so precariously that one can't help but wonder if the driver is bracing for the inevitable. Structural engineers would likely be horrified at the sight, yet these overloaded lorries continue to make their way across the country as if nothing were amiss. But in Kenya, resourcefulness is key. Need more space? Just add a few more sacks and call it 'secure.'

ROADS FULL OF IDIOTS

On Kenyan roads, it's not about what a vehicle should carry; it's about what it can. Why adhere to safety limits when you can push the boundaries of engineering? Whether it's a Bodaboda carrying sofa set or Matatu overloaded with people and goods the daily sight on Kenyan roads is an ongoing test of the limits of what's possible and at times, what's reasonable.

So the next time you find yourself dodging potholes, squeezing past a Matatu packed beyond belief, or marveling at a Bodaboda balancing a gas cylinders, just remember: in Kenya, overloading is not a mistake, it's an art form.

Chapter 15: Road Signs

In theory, the Kenyan road network is governed by something called the Highway Code, a collection of rules and regulations that is supposed to ensure that traffic flows smoothly and safely. Now, if you've ever driven in Kenya, you might have had the distinct feeling that the Highway Code is more of a suggestion, an abstract ideal, like 'peace on earth' or 'unlimited internet data.' Sure, it's there, and sure, it's officially on the books, but in reality, it's not something that people really follow. It's like the recommended 5 daily serving of vegetables and fruits; you know it's important, but when it comes down to it, most people skip it and just get on with their day.

You see, Kenya's version of the Highway Code is remarkably similar to the UK's, with rules about speed limits, lane discipline, and the like. There are even signs for things like stop, yield, and pedestrian crossings, you know, the ones that are supposed to keep everyone alive and relatively unharmed as they make their way from point A to point B. But here's the twist: nobody follows them.

Let's start with the speed limits. There are signs that tell you how fast you're supposed to go, but they might as well be Let's be honest, if you're driving in Kenya, the speed limit is more of a suggestion than a rule. It's not just the Matatus, either; even personal cars are guilty of this. The only time a driver might slow down to follow the limit is to avoid a massive pothole or because they're trying not to hit a police officer who's frantically waving them down. If an ambulance is speeding through, miraculously, everyone will give way, but you can bet that someone will follow right behind the ambulance, matching its speed. For them, it's not about helping the emergency; it's just a chance to move faster since everyone else is clearing the road.

And those road signs? Oh, they're certainly there, scattered around the place like little beacons of order, desperately pleading for some attention. You've got the stop signs, but the drivers just roll right through them without a second thought, because why stop when you can speed up? After all, the traffic behind you is waiting, and the real race is you getting to your destination.

Some of the more confusing road signs are the ones that seem to have been designed with the assumption that everyone has passed some sort of basic driver's education. But here's the thing: many Kenyan drivers have never actually been to driving school. The driving license is often handed out after a quick test of patience (and some bribery, if we're being honest), but that doesn't mean the person actually knows what a yield sign is, let alone a no parking zone. For many, it's a mystery that exists only in theory, much like the idea of a well maintained road.

In fact, it's not uncommon for people to drive around with a brand new license and no real understanding of what any of those road signs mean. They may have learned how to parallel park once or twice but the intricacies of navigating a roundabout or deciphering the complicated rules of a pedestrian crossing are way beyond them. And don't even get me started on the highway code itself, most drivers wouldn't recognize it if it hit them in the face. Some may not even know what a 'one way' sign means, and even fewer know why a 'no overtaking' sign exists when overtaking is basically a national pastime.

But it's not just the ignorance of the rules that makes the road signs so entertaining, it's also the lack of maintenance. You know those nice, reflective signs that tell you to 'slow down' or 'stop'? Well, in Kenya, many of them end up being recycled. Vandalized, too. It's not unusual for road signs to mysteriously disappear overnight, and no one quite knows where they've gone, except maybe the local Jua Kali craftsman who has found a new, lucrative use for them. Yes, some of those missing road signs have been repurposed into all sorts of incredible creations, including but not limited to knives, scoops, and fancy metal sculptures. It's not just a lack of respect for the rules of the road, it's a full blown road sign black market!

Take the stop signs, for example. You don't exactly find them in the Jua Kali shops, but somehow, most Kenyans know where they go. These signs are taken from their posts and repurposed for everything from homemade knives to household tools. You'll never find them neatly displayed for sale, but ask around, and you'll hear stories about how these signs end up in the hands of skilled artisans, who turn them into sharp kitchen knives capable of cutting through the toughest meats. Once a symbol of order at a busy intersection, the sign is now a tool for life's more practical challenges. It's a testament to Kenya's resourcefulness, though it does make you wonder why we bother putting up road signs in the first place if they're only going to end up as scrap or cooking utensils.

And those signs that do manage to stay up? Well, you will never see one that says 'Caution: Cattle Crossing.' There is no cattle neatly crossing at designated spots. Instead, the Maasai cows, grazing by the road, will wander and cross the road wherever they please, and all the vehicles must slow down, dodging cows casually strolling or running across the road. As for the 'Slippery Road' sign, it's pretty much irrelevant as when it rains, the whole road turns into a slippery mess, no matter what the sign says if there is any.

Now, let's talk about those mysterious bump signs, the ones that warn you about upcoming bumps or undulating road surfaces. They're supposed to prepare you for what's coming, but in Kenya, these signs seem to serve more as a suggestion. You'll see one a few meters ahead of a gaping hole in the road, and even though you've been warned, it's like the bump is on a mission to make sure you forget about everything you knew about suspension systems. The hole is always larger than expected, and the bump is often a surprise because 'pothole' is more accurate than 'bump.'

And let's talk about those massive bumps that suddenly appear in the middle of highways like Thika Road, or the new ones that seem to pop up without any warning signs. It's like a magic trick, just when you think the road is smooth, a mysterious bump appears out of nowhere, as if reminding you that roads in Kenya are never predictable. They may not always be convenient, but they sure keep you on your toes and make the journey far more entertaining.

The road signs you see in Kenya may or may not actually be there when you need them. Even when they are, it doesn't guarantee that drivers understand or obey them. For example, you will not spot a sign indicating "Cattle Crossing," In reality, cattle often wander wherever they please.

If the signs are there they often lack the clarity and enforcement needed to ensure the safety of everyone on the road. This is a serious issue, as road safety depends on both effective signage and the willingness of drivers to respect those signs.

Chapter 16: Bodaboda Wars: Bikes vs. Cars

The roads in Kenya are like a giant stage, and every day, a new battle unfolds between two of the most formidable warriors: the cars and the Bodabodas. It's not just traffic, it's a turf war, a contest for road supremacy where no one backs down. Picture it: Matatus jostling for position, Bodabodas weaving through traffic like a swarm of bees, and cars doing everything they can to hold onto their lane as if their life depended on it. Who will emerge victorious in this never, ending struggle? It's always up for debate, because in Kenya, the winner isn't always who you think.

Alright, let's talk about Bodabodas, the fearless, two-wheeled daredevils of the streets! These guys are everywhere, zipping between lanes, squeezing through gaps. They glide through traffic like Nairobi ninjas, dodging cars and Matatus with a level of precision that'll make you question how they're not crashing every second. But it's not just about speed it's like a wild, chaotic dance. Bodaboda riders somehow pull off miracles, weaving through spaces that barely fit a bicycle, let alone a full-on motorcycle. It's an art, requiring mad skills, a love for danger, and, let's be honest, a complete lack of regard for the rules!

Now, enter the cars, the seasoned road warriors with their windows up and drivers muttering under their breath as they try to maneuver through the mess. They've got the horsepower, the fancy gadgets, and, supposedly, the right of way. But there's one thing they don't have: space. And when you're behind the wheel of a car, navigating Kenyan towns and city streets, you quickly realize that space is a luxury you can't afford. Bodabodas don't have that problem. They're always one move ahead, and that's what drives car drivers' crazy. Cars and Bodabodas occupy the same road, but they live in two completely different realities.

And that's when things start to get interesting. Cars are often 'king of the road', they claim the lanes, they have the size, and they feel entitled to their own little territory. But the Bodabodas? They're like sharks in a fish tank, always moving, always hunting for that next gap. A Matatu might try to cut in, a traffic jam will form, and yet, the Bodaboda remains calm, slipping past it all like a water snake, effortlessly cutting through the chaos.

This, of course, leads to drama. The Bodaboda riders don't respect the traditional flow of traffic, they're rebels. When a car decides to pull out into the lane without warning, the Bodaboda is already there, revving its engine and demanding the road with an almost cocky sense of entitlement. And don't even think about turning left or right even with signaling, the Bodaboda is already next to you, giving you the sort of look that says, 'Nice try, but I'm already on the other side of you.' It's a game of chicken, but the car doesn't stand a chance.

On the flip side, cars tend to have a bit more swagger. They honk, they flash their lights, and they make those sharp lane changes that scream 'I own this road.' But when it comes to a Bodaboda cutting in front of them, right in the blind spot, mind you, it's an entirely different story. There's a moment of panic, a rapid swerve to avoid the inevitable crash, and a very loud honk of frustration. But the Bodaboda rider? He doesn't flinch. He's too busy dodging traffic like it's a video game, laughing at the chaos he's just caused and completely unfazed by the fact that he's a hair's breadth away from death.

But the real drama unfolds at intersections. This is where the true war begins. The car approaches the intersection, waiting for the light to turn green, but the Bodaboda sees an opportunity. He doesn't have time for traffic lights. He's seen the green man, the red man, and the yellow man, and none of them scare him. He's beyond rules, he's a force of nature, and he's going for it. He weaves through the queue of stuck cars, making his move like a fast, moving shadow. He's the hero, the trickster, and the villain, all at once. To him, the road is his, and everyone else is just standing in his way.

There's a special kind of pride that comes with being a Bodaboda rider. They're the unsung heroes of urban transport. Their traffic, defying skills are legendary, and their ability to survive through impossible maneuvers deserves a standing ovation. They're always in a rush, always fighting to get ahead, but it's not just the destination that matters, it's the journey. It's about being first, about showing the world that you are the king of the streets, the underdog that manages to beat the odds.

But don't let the Bodaboda riders fool you, there's a lot of risk in this game. Sure, they dodge cars and Matatus like they were born to do it, but a single wrong move could send them flying. The road may be their battleground, but it's also their graveyard. And yet, despite the danger, they don't seem to care. They're here to win this battle, and they'll stop at nothing to claim their victory.

On the flip side, the cars have their own form of defense: horns. While Bodabodas are making their moves through tight spaces, cars are leaning on their horns like it's a national pastime. Horns are used to express rage, frustration, or, if you're a Matatu, sheer excitement at the prospect of getting to your destination five minutes sooner.

But the truth is, both sides are locked in an eternal standoff. The cars will continue to dominate the lanes, while the Bodabodas will forever be the nimble acrobats darting around them. The horn battles will rage on, the swerve and dodge will continue, and neither side will ever completely win. It's a never, ending war, a chaotic, hilarious, and sometimes life, threatening game of dodgeball on two wheels and four.

As the traffic light turns red once again and both sides prepare for another round, one thing is certain: The Bodaboda and the car, despite all their differences, will always share the same road. And in Kenya, no one ever truly gets out of the battlefield unscathed.

Chapter 17: The Roundabout Gamble

If you ever want to experience chaos and confusion in one beautifully disorienting package, look no further than Kenya's roundabouts. These dizzying, circular road features are supposed to provide a seamless flow of traffic, allowing cars to move with the elegance of a carefully choreographed ballet. In theory, that is. In practice, they're more like wild, spinning death traps, a place where logic, road signs, and the highway code go to die.

Now, let's start with the basics. Roundabouts are designed with one simple rule in mind: give way to traffic coming from your right. Simple, right? In theory, this is a foolproof system. You approach the roundabout, you stop, check for traffic from your right, and proceed if it's safe. But this is Kenya, where theory and practice don't always align. In reality, no one has any idea who has the right of way, and everyone just makes it up as they go along.

It's almost like stepping onto a spin the wheel game, except instead of a giant wheel, you're surrounded by honking Matatus, Bodabodas, and an occasional pedestrian who has decided that the roundabout is a footpath. There are no rules here, only instincts and bravery, and perhaps a healthy dose of luck.

The thing about Kenya's roundabouts is that they look simple from a distance. You approach, and for a moment, you think, 'Okay, I got this. It's just a circle.' But then, the madness begins. Matatus come at you from every direction, cutting across lanes like they're auditioning for a stunt scene in a Hollywood action movie. Bodabodas will zip through gaps that you didn't even know existed, weaving in and out of traffic like they're in an obstacle course designed by a madman. And cars? They'll be overly confident, believing that the roundabout is their kingdom, and anyone who dares enter it without the proper respect will be pushed off the road.

But what really makes this a roulette is the lack of order. At any given moment, you might be driving straight into the path of a vehicle that seems to have appeared out of thin air. Drivers don't follow the rules; they just assume that whoever can force their way through first wins. Who has the right of way? That's the million, dollar question, and honestly, it's anyone's guess. Sometimes, it feels like it's a matter of who honks loudest or who has the biggest vehicle. If you're in a Bodaboda, you'd better pray your brakes work because no one else seems to care.

It's a game of survival. The only strategy? Go in with confidence, don't hesitate, and pray to all the gods that you don't end up causing a pile, up. At least that's the mentality most drivers adopt. Matatus treat the roundabout like their personal racetrack, zipping around with no regard for lane discipline or speed limits. It's as if they believe they're on a mission to prove that they're faster than the law of physics. They take the sharpest turns, dart between vehicles, and honk incessantly as if their horn is some sort of charm that will clear the path.

Meanwhile, the cars inside the roundabout are equally frenzied. If you're not aggressive enough, you'll be trapped on the roundabout forever, circling like a hamster on a wheel. If you're lucky, you'll find a small gap and escape without anyone shouting at you or honking. But that's not always the case. Traffic lights and road signs? Don't even bother. They're like a theoretical concept, something you read about in books but have never actually seen in action. Rules? Pfft. They're for people who have the luxury of following them, but in a roundabout, anything goes.

But let's not forget the pedestrians, who have their own special brand of chaos to contribute. Pedestrians crossing in and out of the roundabout add an extra layer of excitement. With no footpaths, they might choose to walk right through the middle of the roundabout. Forget trying to figure out when it's safe to cross, it's always an adventure. The pedestrian is like a wildcard, moving across lanes like they're walking in a park, completely unaware that they're playing an unofficial game of chicken with the moving traffic.

There's also a special breed of hustlers who operate in the roundabout. They've honed their craft to perfection. These are the street vendors, the hawkers, the opportunists who see an idle car and know it's their moment to shine. As cars inch forward, jammed at the roundabout, the vendors stroll through the chaos, offering everything from water bottles, to sunglasses, to fried chicken. It's like a mobile marketplace, a miniature version of Nairobi's downtown hustle, except it's happening in the middle of a roundabout.

But let's talk about the real game, changer: the police officers stationed at major roundabouts. You might think they're there to regulate the madness, to ensure order. Well, think again. Their role is more like that of an overwhelmed referee in a cage fight, blowing their whistles in vain while everyone continues with their own version of the rules. They stand in the middle, attempting to direct traffic, but their hand signals are more like suggestions than actual commands. And sometimes, as if to add a bit of spice to the drama, you'll notice the police officers honk along with the rest of the traffic, as if they too are part of the roundabout chaos. It's as if they've decided, 'Why fight it? Let's just join in!'

And the roundabout itself? Well, it's not built for pedestrians, nor is it particularly forgiving. It's a test of endurance, a place where, once you enter, you need to hold your breath and pray you don't make a wrong move. It's like a never, ending loop, a space that was designed to simplify traffic flow but has somehow turned into the Wild West of Kenyan roads.

So, what do you do if you find yourself approaching a roundabout? It's simple: take a deep breath, trust your instincts, and don't look back. No one else is, and you certainly can't afford to. The roundabout is a free, for, all and if you survive it without any incidents, consider yourself a hero.

But for the rest of us? We'll continue playing the Roundabout dance, hoping for the best, and learning the rules only as we go.

CHAPTER 18: THE ALL, Knowing Tout

Ah, the Tout, the self-proclaimed king of the Matatu world. In Kenya, a Matatu conductor, known as the 'Tout,' is no ordinary being. He is a salesperson, a traffic enforcer, and, at times, even an entertainer. If you ever find yourself in a Matatu, you'll quickly realize that the Tout is the master of the ship, even if that ship feels like it's sinking with every sharp turn.

In the beginning, they're all charm and smiles, their voices smooth as they herd passengers into the van like cattle, urging you to get in with promises of a quick and cheap ride. They're usually calling out the destinations in rapid fire: 'Nairobi Town, Kenyatta Market, Gikambura, Kiambu, come on, hop in!' Their tone is an art form, so energetic that it's borderline hypnotic, like they're promising you the trip of a lifetime, which, at first, seems true. But once you're inside, the charm quickly fades.

The moment you hand over your fare; they transform from smooth operators to something else entirely. No longer are they the friendly, welcoming figures who ushered you into the vehicle; once that money is in their hands, they become rude, aloof, and almost unrecognizable. As soon as you step in and your fare is accepted, you enter a different zone, a place where you no longer exist as a human being with questions or needs, but just another fare, paying entity to be transported from Point A to Point B.

The rudeness is on another level. Have you ever tried to ask a Tout for your change when you've handed them a bigger note? Good luck. Your polite request will be met with an eye roll, a muttered grumble, and sometimes, a sarcastic response. It's as if you've committed a mortal sin simply by asking for the change that's rightfully yours. You might hear a sharp, 'Eh, the money's small, no need to complain, you should've brought the exact fare!' Or, if you're feeling especially brave and ask too many questions, you'll be met with something more colorful like, 'Hii si kitu ya kumakinikia!' (This isn't something you need to be concerned with!).

And if you dare ask to be dropped at a specific location, oh boy. The moment you mention your drop, off point, the Tout will look at you like you've just asked them to solve world hunger. Suddenly, they are in a hurry to get to the next passenger, to make a few extra shillings by picking up someone on the next street. You could be half, way to your stop, but you'll get an answer like, 'Mimi nitashuka wapi? Eeh, Niko na kazi, wacha tu!' (Where do you expect me to stop? I've got a job to do!). Patience? Forget it.

Once the fare is paid, they don't care if you're packed into the back like sardines or if your bag is being squashed against the window by an oversized backpack. They'll step back with zero empathy, just ensuring their next destination is as crowded as possible. It's a speedy game for them, they need to make sure they fill up the vehicle as quickly as possible and then get to the next stop to repeat the process, again and again.

Forget being nice. If you try to ask for something that inconveniences them in the slightest, you'll see the dark side of the Tout's personality. 'Unaeza sema,' (you can say), they'll quip with a dismissive wave, as if you're interrupting their busy schedule. These are the same people who, moments ago, were all over you with big smiles, offering you a seat in the crowded Matatu, now acting like they don't exist.

And heaven help you if you're the one who made the mistake of not having enough cash for your fare. The moment the Tout realizes this, they might give you a look that could melt ice, and then say something like, 'Sasa, shuka utembee (get out and walk). This is not a free ride!' It's as if you've committed the ultimate crime, how dare you get in without the correct fare.

One of the biggest absurdities of Matatu culture is that, despite the complete lack of customer service, the Tout has an uncanny ability to get away with it all. You'll still need to give them your fare, sit through the ride, and hope that they'll drop you at your desired stop. Meanwhile, the radio is blasting, the Matatu is packed beyond capacity, and your Tout is busy making snide comments to the driver about how slow they're going or how they're not making enough hustle points for the day.

If you're lucky enough to get to your stop without any further confrontation, count yourself blessed. But even if you're just trying to be dropped off at a seemingly normal place, you'll often be met with nasty remarks. 'Mambo ni ya haraka, hatuna time ya wakuwaste!' (We don't have time to waste, hurry, just get off). Your only option is to give in, swallow your pride, and be grateful for the ride. Even though it was anything but pleasant, the next customer will probably deal with worse.

But let's be honest. The reality is that despite all their rudeness, despite all the unanswered questions, the Touts remain the backbone of the Matatu system. Their antics, though frustrating, keep the wheels turning, both literally and figuratively. After all, who else would you trust to wrangle the most chaotic form of public transportation into some semblance of order? Who else would make sure everyone is stuffed into a tiny space, cheek, to jawbone, like a can of sardines?

So, the next time you climb aboard a Matatu, brace yourself. The Tout is no longer your friend once you hand over your fare. He is your ticket to the wild ride ahead, and maybe, just maybe, if you're lucky, he will even let you live through the experience without throwing in an extra insult or two.

Chapter 19: Surviving the Sakaja

In Kenya, there are rules, and then there are the rules that never seem to matter. Nowhere is this more evident than when you step into the world of Sakaja, or as the locals call it, the Matatu and Bodaboda's battleground. The government may pass laws with the elegance of a high, speed train, but in the world of Kenyan transportation, it's more like a dodgy old Matatu: loud, unreliable, and filled with more drama than you'd ever imagine.

Let's start with the Matatus. They're supposed to obey the rules, at least according to the glossy pamphlets they hand out at the traffic offices. But the reality? Matatu drivers and Touts have taken a lifelong vow to bend or outright ignore every regulation ever written. Just ask them about the designated parking areas for their vehicles and they'll look at you like you've asked them to explain quantum physics. The law might say they shouldn't be in certain areas, but the Matatu drivers have perfected the art of squeezing into places that were never meant for a vehicle the size of a small country.

But then, let's talk about the Bodabodas. Ah, the Bodaboda culture, a thriving, fearless, and wonderfully chaotic part of Kenyan life. The rules around them are clear as day: they're not supposed to enter the Central Business District (CBD). But here's the twist, every day, like clockwork, these fearless two, wheelers sashay into the CBD as though the law didn't exist. In fact, the one thing more predictable than a Bodaboda weaving through traffic is the discovery that it will likely be found right in the heart of the CBD, parked neatly between taxis and food vendors, waiting to pick up its next brave soul.

In theory, Bodabodas aren't supposed to be allowed in the city center, thanks to a government regulation aimed at easing traffic congestion and preventing further chaos on already crowded streets. The idea is simple: keep the motorcycles out, and maybe, just maybe the roads will be less of a nightmare. But calling this rule anything more than a mere suggestion would be a grave mistake. Just ask any Bodaboda rider, and they'll tell you straight up: "The rules are for those who want to get stuck in traffic."

For them, it's all about survival, hustling to make a living, no matter what. They've mastered the art of squeezing through gaps, darting between cars, and weaving through traffic like they own the road. And while the rest of us are stuck waiting for lights to change or inching forward in gridlocked lanes, the Bodaboda riders move through it all with a confidence that borders on defiance. They see themselves as the lifeblood of the city, the unsung heroes who get people from point A to point B without waiting for hours.

It's a delicate balance of necessity and rebellion, a game of urban maneuvering that's both daring and efficient. While some might call it reckless, they view it as just another day in the life of a hustler trying to make an honest living in a city where time is money. And in the hustle and bustle of city life, subtlety is their specialty. No loud announcements, no signs of defiance just a quiet, practiced glide through the madness, proving that the rules are only as important as the people willing to follow them.

So, what happens when these two forces, the Matatus and the Bodabodas decide to push the limits of the law? Enter the Askari, the city council enforcers who are supposed to ensure the rules are actually followed. Now, the Askari are a different breed altogether. They carry the power to make life difficult in a hurry, from issuing hefty fines to toying vehicles off the road, all with a look that could freeze anyone in their tracks. Picture a small, often grumpy figure, decked out in uniform, striding confidently with a baton ready to dish out consequences to anyone bold enough to defy the law.

These enforcers aren't exactly the same as the traffic cops, but there's one key difference: they have a flair for the dramatic. Where a simple warning might do, an Askari will turn the situation into a spectacle, waving their baton, shouting commands, and making sure everyone within earshot knows that they're in charge. It's not just about following the law; it's about creating a scene, as if to remind everyone that they're the authority in this game of urban chaos. The drama is part of the job, making the enforcement of traffic rules feel more like a theatrical performance than a straightforward task.

It's like they went to a special school called 'How to Make Everyone Miserable While Wearing a Badge'. They can stop you mid, traffic, in the middle of an intersection, with a look that could melt steel, and then proceed to berate you for doing something that everyone around you is doing. It's not just about stopping violations, it's about making sure you know you've been caught, and making sure everyone around you knows it, too.

But let's get to the real entertainment. Government crackdowns on rogue Matatus and Bodabodas are meant to strike fear into the heart of any lawbreaker. After all, getting caught could mean hefty fines, impoundment, and the added embarrassment of a very public scolding. But in reality, these crackdowns are often nothing short of comedic gold.

Take the Matatus, for example. Every time there's a crackdown, they spring into action with a whole arsenal of defensive moves. The first line of defense? Declaring a "Matatu strike." They know full well that the masses depend on them to get to work, and the city can't run without them. The public outcry is swift, the pressure on the government mounts, and before long, the authorities cave. The Matatus get what they want, and the crackdown fizzles out, leaving behind a trail of frustrated commuters and an unshaken fleet of Matatus back to business as usual. It's a masterclass in negotiation, drama, and the undeniable power of public demand, all rolled into one.

And the Bodabodas? Well, they've mastered the art of avoidance. The moment the Askari appear, it's like a magical dance of dodging, Bodaboda riders will dart into alleyways, squeeze through non, existent gaps, or simply vanish into thin air. It's like a game of hide and seek, and the Askari are always the ones who lose. Of course, when they're not avoiding arrest, they're still picking up passengers in areas that are clearly off limits all while making sure to rev their engines as loudly as possible to annoy everyone within a 10-mile radius.

THE ENTIRE SYSTEM IS a dance of defiance. The traffic police maybe there, they may wave their hands in despair, but the drivers are still driving with impunity, laughing all the way to the next corner. Despite all the mayhem, the rules, and the crackdowns, the roads still go on. The roads of Kenya are like a living, breathing organism, a beast of chaos, creativity, and resilience. And when the government crackdown is over, it's business as usual, Matatus are back on the roads, Bodabodas are back in the CBD, and the Askari are, well, probably taking a well, deserved nap until the next crackdown arrives.

After all, rules are just guidelines, aren't they?

Chapter 20: The Terminal Tyrants

Beneath the chaotic surface of Kenya's bustling Matatu and bus terminals lies a shadowy underworld, a world where the real traffic rules are made not by the government or traffic police, but by the cartels that control these spaces. It's a world that makes the normal road rage seem like a child's tantrum, and one that's as dangerous as it is deeply ingrained in the day to day functioning of public transport.

If you've ever been to a terminal, you've probably noticed something strange: the bustling crowd, the endless rows of Matatus, the scattered vendors, and the haggling touts. But what you don't see is the real power, the terminal gangs. Oh yes, behind every corner of those seemingly innocent terminals lurk groups of people who hold absolute power. These are the Terminal Tyrants, ruthless figures who govern everything from how much you'll pay to get to your destination, to whether your Matatu will make it onto the road in the first place.

The process is simple: every Matatu driver must pay their 'protection fee', or they risk having their vehicle vandalized, stolen, or simply locked out of the terminal. Forget the idea that filling up a vehicle is just about collecting passengers, it's also about making sure that the cartel allows you to pick up passengers at all.

The protection fees can range from a small sum to an astronomical amount, depending on the routes being operated. It's like an unofficial toll system where the price of the toll increases based on the popularity of the route. Want to go from Nairobi to Nyeri? That'll cost you a tidy sum, and good luck if you try to compete with another gang, controlled terminal. And if you try to dodge payment, you'll quickly find that nothing is more dangerous than a Matatu boss's anger.

And let's not even get started on the rival gangs. There's a term in Nairobi's Matatu circles that every driver knows: 'Terminal wars'. These are not the typical gang wars you read about in the papers. No, this is a special breed of confrontation, where rival gangs, often armed with screwdrivers, sticks, and body mass, duke it out for terminal dominance. The result is often an unholy spectacle, with Matatus caught in the crossfire, ripped seats, shattered windows, and, if you're unlucky, a bit of blood on the pavement.

Despite the chaos and the intimidation, the system operates with surprising efficiency, largely due to the organized structure of the designated parking spots. These spots are not just areas where vehicles park; they are strategically important and heavily contested. Each Matatu and bus is required to pick up passengers from specific, regulated areas, and they cannot simply park wherever they please. These parking zones are controlled by associations, and drivers must align with certain groups to gain the privilege of picking up passengers. It's a business, and access comes with a price.

In the Matatu terminals, the system may be noisy and chaotic, but there's a surprising level of order, especially when it comes to parking. Every vehicle, regardless of size or status, has a designated spot. As long as they've paid the required fee, they're treated fairly. The rivalry for these spots can be fierce, with drivers sometimes getting into heated arguments over who gets to park where, but it's always about securing their rightful space, not trying to push others out. The system works, and as long as everyone plays by the rules and pays their dues, they all get their fair share of the action. Inside the terminals, the bosses hold authority, but they make sure that every vehicle, big or small, gets a fair chance to pick up passengers. Want to play music in your Matatu? If you're following the rules, no one will stop you. It's a loud, busy world, but there's a surprising sense of fairness as long as you pay the price and stick to your designated spot.

The Terminal Tyrants are the unseen hands that keep the wheels of Kenya's public transport system turning. They are the true puppeteers, pulling the strings behind the scenes, and without them, the whole system would collapse into chaos. Despite their ruthlessness, though, they are necessary evils, like the chaotic cogs that make the Matatu machine run smoothly (if you can call it that).

In the end, whether you're a Matatu driver, a passenger, or just someone trying to get from one place to another, the key to survival in the terminal underworld is simple: know who's in charge, keep your payments up to date, and stay out of the way when the gang war begins. Because in these terminals, everyone has their price, and if you're not careful, you might just find that you're the one who pays it.

Chapter 21: Rain, Rain, Chaos Again

In Kenya, rain isn't just a natural phenomenon, it's an event. A transformative force that holds the country in a grip of madness, turning even the most ordinary commute into a battle for survival. When those dark, heavy clouds gather in the sky, it's not just the weather that changes, it's everything. People brace for what feels like the inevitable catastrophe that is about to unfold.

The roads, already in a state of disrepair, immediately turn into rivers. The potholes, which already serve as mini craters, now morph into lakes that could easily drown your vehicle up to its axles. And let's not even talk about the flooded pedestrian paths, or rather, the complete lack of them. The few pedestrians brave enough to face the elements find themselves wading through murky, brown torrents that would make any seasoned swimmer reconsider their life choices. But in Kenya, even the most seasoned pedestrian has no choice but to brace the waters, the alternative is standing on the side of the road forever, hoping for a break.

It's a commuter's nightmare, but for some, it's the ultimate business opportunity. The touts, those ever, present figures in the Matatu world, know one thing for certain: when it rains, the desperate are easy targets. Fares skyrocket as if by magic, a journey that costs you a modest 50 shillings on a sunny day suddenly demands 200 shillings. And the touts, who seem to multiply in number the moment the first drop of rain falls, start shouting their pitch: 'Hii ni express!' (This is express!).

The irony, of course, is that the so, called 'express' Matatus are stuck in the same traffic jam as the rest of us. No one is going anywhere fast, not in this downpour. But that doesn't stop the touts from selling their dream of speed and comfort. They will happily squeeze you into a packed Matatu and promise you a seat by the window, only for you to end up sitting in a pool of floodwater as you inch along at snail's pace.

Meanwhile, the roads become a game of survival for drivers. Cars, already battered by years of neglect, struggle to stay afloat in the rising waters. The heavy rains expose the pitfalls of Nairobi's infrastructure; potholes are now swimming pools, and the floodwater pours into streets faster than it can drain away. The traffic lights, typically already non, functional, become unreadable blurs as they're swallowed by the relentless rainfall.

Drivers lose all sense of direction, literally and metaphorically. The honking becomes louder, more frantic. Every motorist suddenly thinks they are the only one who knows where they are going, and they're not afraid to let everyone know it. The horns blare as vehicles try to inch forward through swamped intersections, creating an atmosphere that's more akin to suffocating chaos than orderly traffic.

But for pedestrians, the battle doesn't stop at just trying to get a ride. Umbrella vendors, who only moments ago were quiet, suddenly appear out of thin air, each brandishing an umbrella that's more likely to flip inside out than shield you from the torrential downpour. They have the perfect pitch, charging you a premium price for a flimsy piece of plastic that won't last longer than five minutes in the gale, force winds. For those lucky enough to grab one, it's still an uphill battle. The wind joins in the chaos, tearing at the flimsy umbrellas like it's part of the storm's vendetta. The rest of us get to experience the rain directly, with our shoes sacrificed to the watery abyss as the gutters overflow with more debris and refuse than we care to admit.

In the midst of it all, the Bodaboda riders (motorcycle taxi drivers) are having the time of their lives. As traffic comes to a standstill and people are stranded at bus stops, the Bodaboda becomes the holy grail of transport. For a hefty fare, riders will happily ferry you across flooded roads, often with you clinging to their back as water splashes up from all sides. These brave souls are the unsung heroes of the rainy season. Whether it's crossing over mini rivers, skirting around swamped puddles, or simply offering a shortcut through streets no car can pass, they make a killing. But it's a high risk game, and their passengers hold on for dear life, not just from the splashes of water, but from the near death experiences that come with navigating through traffic at top speed in the rain soaked chaos.

As the rain continues to pour down, the city begins to feel like a bizarre carnival. People are now haggling for rides, bribing touts, and trying to stay dry while getting nowhere. Drivers argue with each other over who is in the right lane, and everyone else looks like they are permanently stuck in a rainy purgatory. You might find yourself in a Matatu that is now steaming from the inside because of all the trapped humidity, only to realize that it's still stuck in traffic and you're in no better place than when you started.

Will you get home? Who knows. Will you be stranded in a flooded Matatu, left with no other option but to wait for hours for the storm to subside? It's a coin toss. But somehow, in true Kenyan fashion, everyone makes it through. Maybe not dry, maybe not happy, but we all have one thing in common: we survived the madness of the rain chaos, which, somehow, feels like just another day in the everyday absurdity of the Kenyan road.

Chapter 22: When Animals Attack

Kenya's roads are a shared space, and by that, we mean shared with anything and everything that has four legs (and sometimes two or none at all). While you're trying to avoid potholes, rogue Matatus, and Bodabodas, you might just have to steer clear of an uninvited guest: a cow. Or a goat. Or a whole herd of cows. Yes, on a typical day in Kenya, you can find yourself caught in a traffic jam caused not by the typical factors of human chaos, but by a bovine rebellion.

And it's not just any cows, oh no. These are the Maasai cows, and they don't take kindly to the idea that the roads are for cars. You see, for the Maasai, who see themselves as the true guardians of the land, nothing comes before the welfare of their cattle. Nothing. Not even the progress of urbanization, not even the rules of the road, and certainly not traffic laws. When the dry season arrives, and grazing land in the Maasai land becomes as barren as an unused highway, guess where the Maasai decide to go? Yes, you guessed it: Nairobi and any other city where there is some sort of vegetation and water.

Now, you might think that animals like cows would stay away from the big city, right? Surely, there's a law, right? But then, you'd be wrong. The Maasai have their own kind of road code, and it goes something like: 'Nairobi was part of our land, and if there's no grass where we are from, we are grazing wherever we want, thank you very much.' So, when they march their herds into Nairobi, it's like the ultimate protest: 'You've built your fancy roads, but this is OUR land. Now, step aside and let us eat!'

When the cows decide it's time to enter the city, it's not a gentle parade. No, no. It's a full, scale invasion. Imagine driving down Ngong Road, trying to get to work, when suddenly, you find yourself face, to, face with a cattle caravan, led by a Maasai warrior, proudly carrying a stick in one hand and a smile of contentment in the other. The cows are not interested in your commute, and they most certainly don't care about your honking. They are here for one thing: grass. And if that means walking across highways and forcing you to wait for them to leisurely cross the road in front of your car, then so be it. The cows couldn't care less about your day.

It's not just an inconvenience; it's a cultural moment. The cows, with their majestic horns and casual pace, are the true road rulers. Drivers are left to make a decision: Do I risk honking at the cow and facing a Maasai warrior's wrath, or do I wait patiently while the cows lazily munch their way across, as if they have all the time in the world? The answer is clear: You wait. Because if you honk at a Maasai cow, there's a chance you might have to deal with more than just a delay.

And just when you think it's over, the goats come in. Oh yes. While the cows are marching across one road, the goats are roaming all over the place like they own the city, hopping over fences and dodging cars with gymnastic precision. Have you ever tried to navigate through traffic with goats nonchalantly strolling across your path? It's like trying to drive through a street parade, except the goats don't care if you're late, and neither do the monkeys who occasionally pop in, just to make sure you're not getting too comfortable in your lane.

But back to the Maasai. These herders have a level of conviction in their actions that borders on legendary. When they bring their herds into the city, it's not just to feed their cows, it's to make a statement. They're saying: 'We are the original people of this land. We have the right to walk where we please, and we'll move at our pace, not yours.'

And you know what? The most remarkable thing about this whole phenomenon is that Kenyans have learned to live with it. At first, you might be startled when you're stuck behind a herd of cows on your way to the office, but after a while, it becomes just another part of the urban landscape. In fact, you might even start to feel a strange sense of pride. It's like you've become part of this tropical safari where you're both the tourist and the guide, and the animals are just as much a part of Kenyan's streets as the people.

And then, just when you think you've seen it all, someone in the city will make the mistake of trying to 'help'. We all know that one well, meaning driver who attempts to shoo the cows away, like they're misbehaving pets. Here's a tip for them: Never try to hurry a Maasai cow. These cows are not here for your interference, nor your patience. They'll glare at you with eyes that say, 'If you want to get to your meeting, go around. We're not in any rush.'

So, on the rare occasion that you don't get stuck behind the cows, you'll still have the joy of witnessing the cultural clash between the urban chaos and the rural resilience. And when the cows finally move off the road, you're left with a clear, albeit slightly smelly, reminder that Nairobi's roads belong to more than just the vehicles.

Next time you're stuck in traffic, frustrated by the honking, the sweat, and the endless gridlock, remember: it could be worse. You could be stuck behind a herd of Maasai cows, with no end in sight. So, take a deep breath, and laugh along, because in Kenya, the road is always full of surprises.

Chapter 23: Roads Full of Idiots, Or Is It Us?

By now, after everything we've witnessed on the roads, you might be wondering: Are we the idiots? Are we really the ones who deserve the title of 'the most reckless drivers' in the world? Or perhaps, after all this time navigating the wild landscape of Kenyan roads, we've all become a little... part of the madness?

It's easy to point fingers. We've watched Matatus swerve in and out of lanes, seemingly with no regard for human life, as if their very mission in life is to prove that fate is a funny thing. We've seen Bodabodas zip through traffic with the finesse of a thousand dodgy movie stunts, carrying people, goats, sofas, and entire families like it's a Sunday stroll. Then there's the classic game of 'who's got the right of way?' at roundabouts, where everyone's in a rush, but no one actually knows the rules.

But let's take a moment to pause and reflect: are they really the idiots? Or is it just us, the people who get caught up in the insanity, the ones who grumble as we watch the madness unfold? The ones who, after all the chaos, sit in the back of a Matatu, crammed between a grandmother, a chicken, and a guy with a basket of mangoes, thinking, 'Well, I could have been home an hour ago if I'd just taken the bus.' But nope. We're all here, in it together, with our shared misery and constant honking.

Let's not forget the delusional optimism we have. You know the feeling. You're sitting in traffic, watching a Matatu make illegal U-turns across three lanes of a congested highway, and you think, 'Ah, this is my chance!' You move to the edge of the road, signal your intent to overtake, and, oh, wait. There's another Matatu doing the same thing on your side of the road. Welcome to the game of 'who can fit into the tiniest space.'

Or what about when the traffic lights finally turn green after what feels like an eternity? Instead of the coordinated, well, oiled machine we imagine, we all set off at the same time, honking, dodging, and swerving like we're in some high speed chase in an action movie. Then, someone inevitably runs the red light and not even in a cool way, like they're in the middle of an emergency. Nope. They just don't feel like waiting. And here we are, shaking our heads and wondering, 'Why is everyone such an idiot?' But we all just did the same thing.

Let's face it: the real question is why do we all do it? Why do we feel compelled to behave like complete lunatics when we get behind the wheel or jump into a Matatu? Maybe, just maybe, it's the culture of chaos that permeates the streets. The unspoken rules that tell us, 'If you're not cutting someone off or playing chicken with another vehicle, then you're just not doing it right.' The road is a big, chaotic stage, and we're all actors in the most absurd performance imaginable. Everyone is a star, but no one has read the script.

The truth is, we might not be all that different from the so, called 'idiots' who make the roads feel like a live action demolition derby. We all make poor decisions, whether it's trying to squeeze that extra bit of space in traffic or swerving into an intersection just because 'there's no one around.' We all have that tiny voice in our head that tells us to skip the line or overtake that slow poke and we listen. Sometimes it works. Most of the time, we end up in a honking standoff with a Bodaboda that's just as frustrated as we are.

But here's the kicker: the chaos is part of the charm. The fact that we all survive these roads often unscathed is a testament to the resilience of the Kenyan spirit. It's not just about dodging potholes or surviving the Matatu DJ's worst playlist. It's about navigating through this world of ridiculousness with a grin and a shake of the head. It's about laughing at ourselves because, in the end, everyone knows that life on the road is one big game of chance. It's only a matter of time before we're all the idiot in someone else's story.

And so, after all is said and done, maybe we should stop calling everyone else 'idiots' on the road. Maybe it's time we accept that we're all in the same boat. We're all trying to get somewhere. We're all a little bit reckless and a lot impatient. But in the grand scheme of things, does it really matter? After all, if we can all laugh at the absurdity of it, we must be doing something right.

So, next time you find yourself stuck in traffic, swearing under your breath, and wondering what kind of road dwelling species the driver in front of you belongs to, take a moment to breathe. Embrace the madness. Enjoy the chaos. And, just maybe, become part of the solution, instead of the problem. Follow the traffic rules, be safe, let others be safe!

Did you love *Roads Full of Idiots*? Then you should read *365 Days of Positivity Quotes* by Asha!

Start every day with a spark of positivity and a dose of inspiration! *365 Days of Empowerment: Daily Affirmations for the Whole Year* is your companion to building confidence, resilience, and inner strength.

This beautiful book offers a collection of daily affirmations designed to uplift your spirit, boost your mindset, and encourage personal growth throughout the year. Whether you're seeking motivation to tackle challenges, peace during hectic moments, or a reminder of your self-worth, these affirmations will guide you on your journey.

Each page is a reminder of your potential and a call to embrace the best version of yourself. Let these affirmations inspire you to take charge of your day, deepen your self-love, and cultivate a life filled with joy, purpose, and empowerment.

Perfect for your bedside, workspace, or daily routine, this book is a thoughtful gift for yourself or anyone looking to start their year with positivity and confidence.

Empower your mind, one day at a time! Get the perfect daily affirmation book for 2025

Also by Asha

The Realm of Echoing Hearts: Adventures Beyond the Veil
The Author's Curse
365 Days of Positivity Quotes
Roads Full of Idiots

www.ingramcontent.com/pod-product-compliance
Lightning Source LLC
LaVergne TN
LVHW091121150826
845673LV00002B/919

* 9 7 9 8 2 3 0 2 6 5 5 6 6 *